Palgrave Macmillan Memory Studies

Series Editors: **Andrew Hoskins** and **John Sutton**

The nascent field of Memory Studies emerges from contemporary trends that include a shift from concern with historical knowledge of events to that of memory, from 'what we know' to 'how we remember it'; changes in generational memory; the rapid advance of technologies of memory; panics over declining powers of memory, which mirror our fascination with the possibilities of memory enhancement; and the development of trauma narratives in reshaping the past.

These factors have contributed to an intensification of public discourses on our past over the last thirty years. Technological, political, interpersonal, social and cultural shifts affect what, how and why people and societies remember and forget. This groundbreaking series tackles questions such as: What is 'memory' under these conditions? What are its prospects, and also the prospects for its interdisciplinary and systematic study? What are the conceptual, theoretical and methodological tools for its investigation and illumination?

Titles include:

Aleida Assmann and Sebastian Conrad (*editors*)
MEMORY IN A GLOBAL AGE
Discourses, Practices and Trajectories

Aleida Assmann and Linda Shortt
MEMORY AND POLITICAL CHANGE

Brian Conway
COMMEMORATION AND BLOODY SUNDAY
Pathways of Memory

Richard Crownshaw
THE AFTERLIFE OF HOLOCAUST MEMORY IN CONTEMPORARY
LITERATURE AND CULTURE

Astrid Erll
MEMORY IN CULTURE

Anne Fuchs
AFTER THE DRESDEN BOMBING
Pathways of Memory 1945 to the Present

Yifat Gutman, Adam D. Brown and Amy Sodaro (*editors*)
MEMORY AND THE FUTURE
Transnational Politics, Ethics and Society

Amy Holdsworth
TELEVISION, MEMORY AND NOSTALGIA

Mikyoung Kim and Barry Schwartz (*editors*)
NORTHEAST ASIA'S DIFFICULT PAST
Essays in Collective Memory

Erica Lehrer, Cynthia E. Milton and Monica Eileen Patterson (*editors*)
CURATING DIFFICULT KNOWLEDGE
Violent Pasts in Public Places

Motti Neiger, Oren Meyers and Eyal Zandberg (*editors*)
ON MEDIA MEMORY
Collective Memory in a New Media Age

Evelyn B. Tribble and Nicholas Keene
COGNITIVE ECOLOGIES AND THE HISTORY OF REMEMBERING
Religion, Education and Memory in Early Modern England

Forthcoming titles:

Anne Fuchs
ICON DRESDEN
A Cultural Impact Study from 1945 to the Present

Owain Jones and Joanne Garde-Hansen (*editors*)
GEOGRAPHY AND MEMORY
Exploring Identity, Place and Becoming

Emily Keightley and Michael Pickering
CREATIVE MEMORY

J. Olaf Kleist and Irial Glynn (*editors*)
HISTORY, MEMORY AND MIGRATION
Perceptions of the Past and the Politics of Incorporation

Palgrave Macmillan Memory Studies
Series Standing Order ISBN 978–0–230–23851–0 (hardback)
978–0–230–23852–7 (paperback)
(*outside North America only*)

You can receive future titles in this series as they are published by placing a standing order. Please contact your bookseller or, in case of difficulty, write to us at the address below with your name and address, the title of the series and the ISBN quoted above.

Customer Services Department, Macmillan Distribution Ltd, Houndmills, Basingstoke, Hampshire RG21 6XS, England

Television, Memory and Nostalgia

Amy Holdsworth

First published 2011 by
PALGRAVE MACMILLAN

Palgrave Macmillan in the UK is an imprint of Macmillan Publishers Limited, registered in England, company number 785998, of Houndmills, Basingstoke, Hampshire RG21 6XS.

Palgrave Macmillan in the US is a division of St Martin's Press LLC, 175 Fifth Avenue, New York, NY 10010.

Palgrave Macmillan is the global academic imprint of the above companies and has companies and representatives throughout the world.

Palgrave® and Macmillan® are registered trademarks in the United States, the United Kingdom, Europe and other countries.

ISBN 978–0–230–24598–3

This book is printed on paper suitable for recycling and made from fully managed and sustained forest sources. Logging, pulping and manufacturing processes are expected to conform to the environmental regulations of the country of origin.

A catalogue record for this book is available from the British Library.

Library of Congress Cataloging-in-Publication Data
Holdsworth, Amy, 1979–
    Television, memory and nostalgia / Amy Holdsworth.
        p.   cm. — (Palgrave Macmillan memory studies)
    Based on the author's thesis (doctoral)—University of Warwick.
    Includes bibliographical references and index.
    ISBN 978–0–230–24598–3
    1. Memory on television.   2. Nostalgia on television.   3. Identity
    (Psychology) on television.   4. Television—Psychological aspects.
    I. Title.
    PN1992.M45H65 2011
    791.4301'9—dc23   2011020969

10   9   8   7   6   5   4   3   2   1
20   19   18   17   16   15   14   13   12   11

Printed and bound by CPI Group (UK) Ltd, Croydon, CR0 4YY

For Alice. In Loving Memory

Contents

List of Figures

Acknowledgements

This project began its life as a PhD thesis completed in the Department of Film and Television Studies at the University of Warwick and funded by the Arts and Humanities Research Council (AHRC). I am especially grateful to Charlotte Brunsdon, who supervised the early stages of this work, for her excellent guidance and support. Elsewhere at Warwick, for their continuing friendship, I would like to thank Tracey McVey, Rachel Moseley, Helen Wheatley, and, although we've all moved on, James Bennett, Malini Guha, Iris Kleinecke-Bates, Chris Meir, Laura Ortiz-Garrett and Sarah Thomas for the fun and distractions as well as the reassurance and solidarity. Special thanks to Faye Woods, who has been a constant source of encouragement across the duration of this project, sharing with me both ideas and research materials.

It is at the University of Glasgow that I have developed this earlier work into a book. I would like to thank all my colleagues in Film and TV at Glasgow for the space and time to complete this project and for providing such a welcoming and supportive atmosphere. In particular, I must thank Dimitris Eleftheriotis for reading and discussing with me drafts of Chapter 3, Michael McCann for his technical wizardry and for keeping me laughing, and Karen Lury for her continuous and much-appreciated insight, inspiration, generosity and guidance. Elsewhere at Glasgow I am indebted to those students who took my honours options on 'Contemporary Television Drama' and 'Television, Memory and the Archive' in 2009/10. The energy and enthusiasm I met with in these teaching experiences helped me to reignite this research.

Thanks to all those who have listened to, commented on, shared ideas and materials, and supported this research. I am particularly grateful to the members of the Midlands Television Research Group, the Northern Television Studies Research Group, Jerome de Groot, Ann Gray, Erin Bell, Jonny Roberts, Lisa Taylor, Emily Marshall, Melanie Hoyes, Kerr Castle and Andrew Hoskins. For both their openness and their insights I am indebted to Iain Logie Baird, Kathryn Blacker, Kate Dunn, Claire Thomas and Sheena Vigors at the National Media Museum in Bradford. I must also extend my gratitude to Catherine Mitchell at Palgrave Macmillan for her expert help and guidance in completing this manuscript.

Finally, for their love and seemingly endless patience, I would like to thank my friends and family, especially the C.C., John Holdsworth and Briony Farr, Janet and John Andelin, Matt and Sam Hayball and my sister, Jessica, who, most importantly, grew up with me watching television and continues to watch what I tell her to.

Extracts from the Introduction and Chapter 5 first published as the article ' "Television resurrections": Television and memory', by Amy Holdsworth, in *Cinema Journal*. 47.3, pp. 137–144. Copyright 2008 by the University of Texas Press. All rights reserved.

An earlier version of Chapter 3 first appeared as 'Who do you think you are? family history and memory on British television' in E. Bell and A. Gray (eds.) *Televising History* (2010, Palgrave Macmillan). Reproduced with permission of Palgrave Macmillan.

Introduction

Television has often been characterised by its 'transience', 'ephemerality', 'forgetability' and even more seriously, it is seen as an 'amnesiac', responsible for the 'undermining of memory'. Television is not only the bad critical object in the academy, but is a bad memory object as well. In her account of the shifts in theories and concerns with memory from modernity to late modernity, Susannah Radstone observes that 'whereas in the nineteenth century, it was the felt break with tradition and the long durée which constituted the temporal aspect of the memory crisis, in the late twentieth century, that crisis is inflected, rather, by the experiences of immediacy, instantaneity and simultaneity' (2000, p. 7). Radstone goes on to reiterate, through Sobchack, that the development of new electronic technologies that 'collapse the distance that previously separated an event from its representation' is in part responsible for the 'deepening' of the memory crisis (ibid.). Andreas Huyssen's *Present Pasts* explores how a contemporary fascination with memory might be viewed as a response to the 'spread of amnesia' in Western society. For Huyssen, 'intense public panic of oblivion' is met by the 'contemporary public obsession with memory' (2003, p. 17). This book offers a way of rethinking television's role at the heart of the memory crisis and its paradoxical memory boom by examining the function of memory and nostalgia on a medium and for a medium that is often seen as a metaphor for forgetting.

Television itself is marked by and generates our obsession with commemoration and anniversaries, through its repetition and continual re-narrativisation of grand historical narratives, for example, of world wars and world cups.[1] It is within these 'new electronic technologies',

1

such as television, that a contemporary fascination with memory becomes evident. As Huyssen writes:

> The turn toward memory and the past comes with a great paradox. Ever more frequently, critics accuse this very contemporary memory culture of amnesia, anesthesia, or numbing. They chide the inability and unwillingness to remember, and they lament the loss of historical consciousness. The amnesia reproach is invariably couched in a critique of the media, while it is precisely these media – from print to television to CD-ROMs and the Internet – that make ever more memory available to us day by day.
>
> (2003, pp. 16–17)

Whilst Huyssen's argument moves on to discuss the relationship between remembering and forgetting and the need to make a distinction, among the excesses of a memory and information culture, between 'usable pasts and disposable data' (2003, p. 18), we might also respond to the need to pay specific attention to media forms and the operations of a contemporary memory culture. Radstone's own assertion that ' "memory" means different things at different times' (2000, p. 3) and her suggestion that we need to pay more attention to the '*specificities* of contemporary preoccupations with memory' (2000, p. 6) must open up medium-specific interrogations of memory. There are two primary concerns that are raised by the relationship between television and memory. The first, illuminated by Huyssen's work, is the role of television within the constitution of contemporary memory cultures, and the second, arguably a more neglected area of investigation, is the role of memory in the operation of specific television cultures. Huyssen states that 'we cannot discuss personal, generational, or public memory separately from the enormous influence of the new media as carriers of all forms of memory' (2003, p. 18). If this is so, then it is essential that we re-evaluate the relationship between memory and television not only as an attempt to understand how memory works but also, in Karen Lury's words, as an 'attempt to understand how television works' (2001, p. 25). What is needed is a re-evaluation that remains respectful of both the specificity and the diversity of television's forms and practices.

David Morley reminds us that 'if television is a visual medium, it is also one with a physical materiality all of its own and a wide range of symbolic functions' (2007, p. 282). This is an understanding that runs across the investigations within this book and is central to the opening chapter. From British sitcom *The Royle Family* (BBC, 1998–) to Japanese horror film *Ringu* (dir. Hideo Nakata, 1998), through a series of examples drawn from television and beyond I consider how television's multiple relationships to memory have been and can be thought through. It is this interplay between television as a visual medium and a material object that is at the centre of my analysis. It is an understanding of television as a domestic object watched within the space of the home that underpins this discussion, and I employ the metaphor of the 'black mirror' to consider multiple forms of reflection inside and outside the home and between the television and its viewer. Contrary to the notion of television as an amnesiac and moving on from the privileging of the news and media event in discussions of television memory, here, television is understood as part of both a material network of memory and a system of everyday memory-making within and in relation to the home and the family.

Chapter 2 seeks further to understand the workings of different forms of television in relation to memory through the investigation of 'moments of return' in television drama and representations of remembering and reflection. At the heart of this chapter is the initial provocation that ignited this project – Fredric Jameson's statement that 'memory seems to play no role in television, commercial or otherwise [...] nothing here haunts the mind or leaves its afterimages in the manner of the great moments of film' (1991, pp. 70–71). Contrary to this statement I consider the patterns of haunting, the play with 'afterimages' and the forms and pleasures of repetition within the dramas I discuss – *Perfect Strangers* (BBC, 2001), *ER* (NBC, 1994–2009), *Grey's Anatomy* (ABC, 2005–) and *The Wire* (HBO, 2002–8) – as evidence of the central role of memory within television's dramatic forms. Here the 'moment' also emerges as a way of approaching and writing about the lengthy and complex narratives of serial drama. Whilst the 'black mirror' allows us to consider a form of reflection which 'brings forth', the notion of reflection employed in Chapter 2 is primarily understood as a looking and a referencing back. It is this backwards and forwards movement, patterns of return and retreat, and the 'ebb and flow' of television that is central to my understanding of the medium and which characterises many of the programmes discussed within this book.[2]

This characteristic is drawn from, in part, television's own explorations of the relationships between past and present. In Chapter 3 I discuss the hugely successful family history documentary format of *Who Do You Think You Are?* (BBC, 2004–), where celebrity investigators explore their own family trees. It is a format that places individual stories in relation to wider social histories, the investigations of which are enabled by forms of post-memory and memory work. The part/whole relations characteristic of serial narrative are explored in Chapter 3 in terms of the relationship between the individual and the collective. *Who Do You Think You Are?* produces an affirmative vision of historical connectivity whereby the individual is seen as part of a wider picture, not as a passive subject but as an active historical agent. These affirmations are understood in relation to the work of memory in the series as, in Alessandro Portelli's terms, a 'permanent labour of connecting',[3] realised through the trope of the journey and the emphasis on discovery. This is promoted as the affirmative discovery of both national identity *and* self-identity, where memory emerges as a form of emotional connection with the past that is explored and exploited by the format. The work on this particular series functions as a case study of television's ability to simultaneously open up and close down the potentials of memory and the investigation of history; what is reaffirmed is its role in the production and reinforcement of patterns of remembering and forgetting.

The dynamics of remembering and forgetting are clearly apparent in the descriptions of the paradoxical 'memory boom'. Whilst television is often viewed as central to this 'postmodern condition' that produces an abundance of memory in response to the fear of forgetting, we might see how television itself is struck by a similar affliction. This is arguably intensified by the acknowledgement of its own immateriality and transience and heightened at a time of dramatic technological change and uncertainty over the future of the medium. Lynn Spigel's observation in *Television After TV* that 'television – once the most familiar of everyday objects – is now transforming at such rapid speeds that we no longer really know what "TV" is at all' (2004, p. 6) illuminates the intensified instability of both television and television studies. Fear that television, the professed medium par excellence for the production of vanishing acts, will itself inevitably disappear might be seen to lead towards an increased obsession with television memory and the nostalgia for television past. Anxieties about television and even television studies, therefore, might be seen to run parallel to present anxieties regarding history and memory in general.

Using the UK example of ITV's celebrations of its fiftieth anniversary in 2005, Stephen Lacey writes that 'television history is in the air and on the screen. It is ironic, perhaps that the broadcasters should be looking back at the point at which the medium is engaged in a process of profound technological and cultural change' (2006, p. 10). This is not necessarily ironic but is a phenomenon that fits into the 'logic' of discussions of contemporary memory culture and points towards television's *own* memory boom; that the medium is now 'lost *in* memory'. Examples of this increased memorialisation of past television within the British context include: the reinvention and resurrection of cult or canonical texts such as *Doctor Who* (BBC, 1963–89; 2005–) or *Life on Mars* (BBC, 2006–7), the popularity of nostalgia programming (i.e. the clip show or list TV) and the scheduling of retrospective seasons (on BBC Four, for example),[4] the phenomenal growth of the TV DVD market and the development of online television archives. These examples of the resurrection of archive television for public consumption also clearly mark the currency of television memory and nostalgia as enabling what Michael Grade, British broadcast executive, has called the exploitation of 'sleeping assets' (in O'Sullivan 1998, p. 202).

The influence of memory studies and the notion of the 'memory boom' prompt a concern with *how*, *why* and to *what effect* memory and nostalgia arise within the televisual landscape and we might read the proliferation of television memory and nostalgia as symptomatic of the current state of television and a response to changes in the medium. However, whilst we lament what has been lost, to employ and rephrase Huyssen's argument, it is precisely these changes – digitisation, DVD, online archives – that make ever more television memory available to us day by day.

It is here that we must call to attention the different national contexts of television memory and nostalgia. Whilst the recirculation of past television has noticeably increased with the emergence of multi-channel and digital television within Britain, the case is entirely different for the North American broadcasting system, where the practice of syndication and the rerun have a long tradition. Derek Kompare's research on the historical development of the rerun on American television examines what he refers to as the 'regime of repetition' – the constant recirculation of the nation's cultural and individual pasts in the present through the ubiquity of past television (2002, p. 19). The revelations of Kompare's study necessitate an examination of *what* is called upon and *when*; to consider the historical and national specificity of television memory and nostalgia. Whilst it is not the intention of this book to translate Kompare's work into a comparative British study, by paying attention to the way in which past television is re-contextualised, through textual, generic, personal and institutional practices, we might begin to investigate the construction of television's *own* memory cultures and our engagement with them.

It is these forms of re-encounter and re-contextualisation that form the centre of my analysis in Chapters 4 and 5. Chapter 4 investigates textual forms of encounter with past television through a study of the relationship between television and nostalgia – a term that is often evoked in relation to television but which has seen little sustained attention to the significance of its meanings for understanding of the medium. At the centre of this discussion is 'television about television' – the list show, the UK and US versions of *Life on Mars* and forms of institutional nostalgia. Self-conscious, playful and paradoxical – nostalgia is explored as a way of approaching television's relationship to and memories of itself, which in turn reveal more about the medium's construction of broader social and cultural memories. Whilst 'television about television' must be seen within a commercial and institutional context, it also reveals much about the potency of generational relationships to television as well as operating within specifically nostalgic forms of longing and reflection.

Chapter 5 returns us to the material cultures of television and examines the re-encounter with the archive through an analysis of the television exhibitions at the UK's National Media Museum (NMM). This particular gallery serves as a case study through which to examine both the potentials and limitations of exhibiting television and as a way of interrogating the long-neglected significance of the medium's materiality, explored in relation to theorisations of the material and memorial cultures of museum practice. As a form of resurrection, curatorial practices and exhibition design reveal much about the ways in which television histories and heritages are constructed but also the ways in which television matters within individual and collective lives through the resonances of memory and nostalgia. The work of curators at the NMM also highlights the real and imaginary material and immaterial cultures of both analogue and digital television – it is this transition between the two that is central to the exploration of a recurring anxiety regarding the end of television. However, as the afterlife of television in the museum illuminates, whilst some might herald the death of television, its past constantly surrounds us, as television's own 'memory boom' expands with the proliferation of television memory technologies and practices. Television is not dead but re-circulates within contemporary culture through a variety of textual, generic, personal and institutional practices. Fredric Jameson once wrote that memory plays 'no role in television' but in the contemporary televisual landscape, memory and nostalgia lie at the very heart.

1

Half the World Away: Television, Space, Time and Memory

This chapter is constructed around a series of examples drawn from cinema, contemporary art and television itself that reveal much about the place of television within the popular imagination. More specifically, each represents a different way in which television's role in the construction of collective and individual memory can be articulated, explored and imagined. It is not an exhaustive compendium of television's multiple relationships with memory – there is still much to be discovered – but an introduction to existing thought and a rethinking of the phenomenological aspects of this relationship; a relationship which finds fruitful lines of inquiry by considering the symbolic functions taken on by television as a visual medium and a material object.

As two ways of approaching television it is this interplay between the visual medium and the material object, between the television text and the context of viewing, that I have found to be a productive way of engaging with and writing about television memories. The majority of the examples I employ are representations of television viewing and each exhibits strong elements of a self-reflexivity which highlights aspects of this interplay. Forms of reflection, central to many parts of this book, emerge as a useful way of exploring television memory in relation to the self, the family, domestic space and the world outside. Characterising the television screen as a form of 'black mirror' produces evocative comparisons between this magical device and the ordinary and overlooked aspects of television as a material object. Television is understood not as a box in the corner of a room but embedded within the sensual aspects of the domestic environment, producing memories which are forged from a network of sense impressions and allowing television to be seen within a network of memories.

Understandings of both space and time have been and continue to be central to conceptualisations of the relationship between television and memory, though it is perhaps the latter which has received the most attention. My first two examples, then, offer different versions of television's temporality and I use them here, at the beginning of this chapter, to respond to what is currently the most extensive area of academic work on television memory.

Marking time: memory and the media event

The various temporalities of television have been somewhat overshadowed by an understanding of 'liveness' as the defining characteristic of the medium, and whilst television's relationship to the ritual and the routine has been much remarked upon there has been little sustained attention to the role of memory within this experience. Digital evolutions in the ways we watch and experience television, inevitably impacting on the ways we remember television, necessitate the re-conceptualisation of increasingly complex relationships between television, time, space and memory. The relationship between analogue and digital experiences and memories of television requires greater investigation both within and beyond the scope of this particular project. I do not wish to draw a line between the two but to suggest that, whilst these digital revolutions intensify the necessity of rethinking understandings of time and memory in relation to television, we might be bolder and challenge, in Mimi White's terms, the 'foundational assumptions' of television theory (2004, p. 76).

The representational modes of the media event (in particular the catastrophic media event), as both breaking news and archive footage, have received much worthy attention.[1] Yet they have come to dominate commentary on television's relationship to memory, producing, as Jerome Bourdon has observed, 'two contradictory models of television memories: a destructive model, and a hyper-integrative model based on a single program type' (2003, p. 6).

The examples I want to employ to consider these two models are both representations of the viewing of media events and both are framed by memory. I use them here to reveal the attitudes towards and the ways in which the relationship between television and time and its affect on memory and experience has been and can be thought through. The first is a sequence from the South Korean film *Oldboy* (dir. Park Chan-Wook, 2003) which highlights postmodern anxieties about television and the impoverishment of experience. The second is a 2008 promo for the

BBC's mobile news service which represents an understanding of television memory in relation to a Western model of linear time and the sequential plotting of history. Memory, here, is also a promotional tool for the BBC, setting up lines of continuity and tradition.

Lost time: *Oldboy*

For Fredric Jameson, television is perceived as being both a bad memory object and a bad critical object. He writes in *Postmodernism* that 'the blockage of fresh thinking before this solid little window against which we strike our heads' is 'not unrelated to precisely that whole or total flow we observe through it' (1991, p. 70). Models of television textuality have long been dominated by Raymond Williams' concept of 'flow' (1974) and it is through this concept that Jameson and others have envisaged television as the producer of lost images and lost time. It is the notion of lost time that is illuminated by the representation of television in the opening scenes of *Oldboy*.

Standing at the edge of the roof of a high building a man in a black suit and with a shock of black hair holds another, leaning off the edge, by his tie. Accompanied by a classic-electro score, so the film begins, powering its way onto the screen. 'I want to tell you my story' the first man proclaims and it is from this point, through flashback, that the events leading to this point are revealed. The man is Oh Dae-Su (Choi Min-Sik), abducted by an unknown kidnapper, for 15 years he has been held captive in a cell that is reminiscent of a cheap hotel room and fed through a hatch in the door, and for 15 years Oh Dae-Su's only companion is the television. This, however, is a hostile and cruel companionship. Powerless and confused, Oh Dae-Su despairingly watches as the television reports his own abduction, his wife's murder and his daughter's disappearance (at the hands of his own captor he must presume). He is teased by the television as his desire for physical connection increases – reaching out to touch the screen, he masturbates to the performance of a female pop star only for the song to end and the programme to cut away before he is satisfied. A false point of connection, television becomes for Oh Dae-Su a way of passing time, and in a montage sequence towards the end of his imprisonment it also becomes a way of marking time for both the director and the audience.

Scratching at the walls with a chopstick, Oh Dae-Su begins an attempt to tunnel out of his cell. As he investigates the potential escape route, the director evokes a sense of the length of time of Oh Dae-Su's imprisonment through the use of a televisual montage and a split screen

Figure 1.1 Split-screen memory in *Oldboy* (dir. Park Chan-Wook, prod. Egg Films/Show East, South Korea, 2003).

(see Figure 1.1). On the left is the dark cinematic image of Oh Dae-Su scraping through and investigating the cavity between the walls then physically preparing himself for freedom. On the right is a televisual montage of key news events occurring in South Korea between 1995 and 2003.[2] The sequence is framed, not by the use of voice-over, as with the rest of the flashback, but by an ambient electronic soundtrack with a steady driving beat.

The sequence sets up a series of tensions and differences through the use of the split screen and by preceding and closing imagery. Representations of television within film often illuminate attitudes towards the former in the popular imagination and by film-makers who often consider it to be an 'inferior' medium. Whilst the split screen might be seen to underline perceived differences between film and television, the treatment of television in the film evokes particular postmodern anxieties regarding the impoverishment of memory and experience. For Geoffrey Hartman, television, and the relentlessness of its flow, produces an 'unreality effect' (2001, p. 113), and it is this derealisation of experience that Oh Dae-Su is seen to battle against.

Within *Oldboy* there is an insistent emphasis on the visceral and the body. Oh Dae-Su's ordeal is worn by his body; his tattooing of his years in captivity upon the back of his hand is contrasted with the use of television to 'mark time'. The real, the authentic and bodily forms of memory (the scars from several suicide attempts and his blistered knuckles from punching the walls) are positioned against the simulated, mediated and artificial. For example, a televised boxing match at the opening of the montage is contrasted with Oh Dae-Su's visceral punch into the camera at its end. Television is emphasised as an unsatisfactory substitute for 'lived' experience and absent of such sensual forms of memory. In Figure 1.1, the coldly lit and dark image of Oh Dae-Su, glistening with sweat as he prepares his assault, is contrasted with the one-dimensional artifice of the graphics of television news. There is also an added violence to the sequence, symbolised by the television, in that it depicts not just time that has passed, but time that is *stolen* from Oh Dae-Su by his captor.

However, the relationship between television and memory functions in an additional way. The sequence works as a marker of time passing not just through the conventions of the news montage but precisely because it relies upon a collective memory of the news events included in the montage. Writing on what he refers to as the 'mediatisation of memory', Andrew Hoskins considers how 'in the conflict-laden field of television news and documentary, highly selected ghosts (e.g. D-Day, the Tet offensive and 9/11) haunt our television screens' (2009, p. 38). Whilst the sequence from *Oldboy* illuminates the national specificity of these 'ghosts', it also highlights the construction of media memory canons as a form of collective television memory. However, the privileging of television news, and specifically the traumatic media event, in critical inquiries on television memory has led to both a polarised commentary, which reproduces models of trauma and therapy, and to the neglect of television's diversity and the various televisual forms, uses and experiences of both memory and nostalgia.[3]

In line with Bourdon's observation on the split commentary of media events, this second example constructs the experience of the media event in a different way, emphasising time as a cumulative experience rather than a vanishing act, and inscribing memories of television within an institutional discourse. Yet it also points towards the re-imagining of the space and place of television within discussions of memory.

The march of time: BBC news promo

In a 1960s living room a crying mother is comforted by her son as she watches news footage of President Kennedy's assassination. In a sunny 1970s caravan park, whilst a young boy plays swingball outside, inside the caravan a young girl, her chin rested on her hands, is absorbed by coverage of Elvis Presley's death on a portable television set (see Figure 1.2). The Berlin Wall is falling and three office colleagues gather around the security guard's television set to watch the celebrations.

Figure 1.2   Remembering watching television news (BBC promo, 2008).

Whilst attending to a patient's intravenous drip a black female doctor watches the release of Nelson Mandela on the television set in a hospital ward lounge. Among the trees and chirping birds a man flicks open his mobile phone, alerted to a new event by the BBC's mobile news service. *Where were you when you heard the news? Where will you be next time?* the strapline asks.

The promo clearly depicts breaking news events as 'moments which can be isolated from the fragmented flow of information, moments with an impact which disrupts the ordinary routine' (Doane 1990, p. 228). It is in the interruption of the routine that these moments have been seen to construct memory rather than disappearing with the rest of television's amnesiac flow. Yet it is a longer view of television that is taken, with the promo presenting a cumulative series of events. Here, the sequential nature of both television and historical time can be emphasised, where televisual flow is characterised by, rather than rupture, a forwards momentum that is mapped onto the march of progress.

Continuity is emphasised by a pattern of shots, and each vignette is constructed through a combination of establishing shot, a medium close-up of the viewer and a close-up of the television set and the news broadcast. These vignettes of viewing are also sutured through the use of sound and music. The merging audio of the archival news reports presents a through-line of voices, each characterised by the received pronunciation of male BBC journalists (Brian Hanrahan and Michael Buerk are seen within the footage) and closing with the voice-over of Mark Strong advertising the service. This is layered with the repetitive and atmospheric refrain of a guitar composition.[4]

For the purposes of the promotion, a highly selective series of 'memorable moments' are chosen, mapping social and political progress (the fall of the Berlin Wall, the release of Mandela) onto the rhetoric of technological liberation; a rhetoric of choice, empowerment and freedom which has been employed across the digital television industry to promote changing services and new forms of viewing. There are clearly symbolic implications to this rhetoric and particularly within this specific promo. For example, we might remark upon the implicit gendering of technology within the sequence, whereby it is the female viewer that is associated with the static analogue set (in the office trio it is the woman with blonde hair, red lipstick and a red suit who stands out within the dark frame) and a male 'viewser' who takes advantage of the freedom associated with the digital era. Whilst I address forms of institutional nostalgia, particularly in relation to the BBC in Chapter 4, we must also remain attentive to the institutional discourses of television memory at work here, as this promo works to stress lines of continuity in the BBC's provision of news and its impact on and address to the viewer as citizen. There is an emphasis upon tradition and continuity in the BBC's news service which soothes rather than aggravates the perceived rupture of digital practices.

Whilst the BBC pats itself on the back for at least half a century of exceptional television news coverage, both impacting upon and weaved into the lives of its viewers, in this example the BBC chooses to employ perhaps one of the most popular and prevalent discourses of television memory which emphasises the role of television as, in Tim O'Sullivan's words, a powerful point of 'symbolic, autobiographical and generational reference' (1998, p. 202) – 'where were you when…?' or perhaps more specifically 'where were you when you watched…?' It is a question which emphasises the significance of place and the context of viewing in memories of television and one which returns us to the importance of the everyday, the domestic, the ritual and the routine in rethinking the complexities of both television and memory and their relationships to the multiple registers of time. It is not my intention to reproduce a familiar binary of linear 'v' cyclical time (see Felski in Radstone 2007, p. 11) but to draw attention to forms of television experience, which, whilst widely remarked upon have produced little conceptual thought in terms of memory. It is the 'where' of the question that I want to open with and then move on to consider television's relationship to domestic space by investigating the various and evocative interplays between text and context through the motif of the mirror and the reflection.

Reflections: memory, the everyday and the domestic

In his short story *Music for Chameleons*, Truman Capote describes how the narrator's gaze is captivated by the magnetic pull of a black mirror: 'My eyes distractedly consult it – are drawn to it against my will, as they sometimes are by the senseless flickerings of an unregulated television set. It has that kind of frivolous power' (2000 [1980], p. 7). Arnaud Maillet (2004) charts the history of the black mirror, its use by artists, magicians and scientists, and its place within Western thought and culture.[5] Here the mirror is an anxious source of suspicion, fear and fascination, in its power to capture and distort the gaze, but also in the possibilities that arise in its reflections – the visions, shadows and phantoms that come forth. More recently, a series of photographs, within artist and academic Svetlana Boym's project 'Nostalgic Technology', employs the reflective surfaces of digital devices – the laptop, the BlackBerry – as 'melancholic black mirrors'.[6] Her evocative description of the interplay of shadows and reflections in her BlackBerry screen, as she travels by train, conjures up a series of tensions and relationships between past and present, virtual and real, modern and *off*-modern.[7] The inactive black screen reflects a decaying post-industrial landscape from the train window, she writes – 'no longer a seductive digital fruit, my blackberry reveals its second life as a melancholic black mirror that brings into sharp focus the decaying non-virtual world that is passing us by'.

It is Capote's connection between the black mirror and the television that I want to return to. Whilst Capote likens the form of autohypnosis produced by the mirror to the electric flickerings of an untuned set, it is the reflective surface of the television screen, both then and now, that I want to draw attention to. Whilst television has been thought of as a 'window on the world' or likened to a mirror, held up to society or reflecting the lives of its audience, it is the idea of the 'black mirror' that I have found particularly evocative. It recalls the shiny smoke-grey glass of the cathode ray television set, and the black lustre of LCD and plasma screens. The former, with its curved and convex screen emitting a distorted and dark reflection of its viewer and setting, and the latter, though less reflective, producing a play of shadows absorbed by the surface.[8]

Unlike the newness and mobility of the 'seductive digital fruit' of Boym's media art, the television is an older, more familiar and commonplace technology. It is also in itself, as object, practice and cultural form, a deeply nostalgic technology. In its most immediate sense and drawn from the etymology of the word, nostalgia is primarily connected to the notion of home. Though I investigate the relationship between nostalgia and television in more detail in Chapter 4, it is this sense of the word that I draw upon here. Wendy Wheeler (1994) has written of nostalgia as a desire for 'being-in-place' and it is this desire that resonates with television's embeddedness in domestic space, the role that television and television memories play in our personal histories, and the way our personal histories are reflected in television. It is these reflections that I want to use to consider television and its relationship to memory as an experience formed over time within the patterns of the everyday. Here, television is remembered and felt as a significant experience that can illuminate histories and memories of the self and the family. The reflections that take place in the black mirror and the television cannot escape the residues of memory – they both bring forth and they look back.

In the mirror the self is held at a distance; it is at once both familiar and strange, close yet half the world away. Boym writes that the black mirror 'sharpens perspective, not framing realistic illusions but estranging perception itself [...] The black mirror offers a different kind of mimesis and an uncanny and anti-narcissistic form of self-reflection.' The reflection is not entirely strange or unfamiliar, but has the potential, as Joe Moran writes of certain kinds of memory, to 'denaturalise the everyday and render it visible' (Moran 2004, p. 57). Like the experience of involuntary memory, catching one's reflection in the television screen produces a form of resonance; the flicker of reflection, the snag of recognition which illuminates that oscillating pattern of the television experience as an 'escape and return to the everyday' (Lury 2007, p. 373).

It is with this in mind that I want to move on to consider a series of examples which might be characterised as reflections, highlighting the relationship between text and context through the motif of the mirror reflection. Each is a self-reflexive representation of the relationship between television and its audience, each presenting a memory of television viewing. The examples are the credit sequence for British sitcom *The Royle Family* (BBC, 1998–), British artist Gillian Wearing's 2006 installation *Family History* and a brief scene from US teen drama *Freaks and Geeks* (NBC, 1999). All are examples that make visible television as an everyday memory-making medium.

Half the world away: *The Royle Family*

Though Anna McCarthy's work on television in public spaces (2003) and an interest in the mobile screens of the digital era (see Dawson 2007) offer an important accompaniment to television's history as a domestic object, television is primarily understood as a domestic medium. Through cultural historical work (see O'Sullivan 1991, Spigel 1992b, Sconce 2000), theoretical investigation (see Silverstone 1994) and qualitative audience studies (see Morley 1986, Gauntlett and Hill 1999, Wood 2009), including the study of soap opera audiences (see Hobson 1982, Ang 1985), television's relationship to the domestic and the routines of the everyday has been extensively researched and theorised. Whilst debates surrounding and accounts of this work are offered elsewhere I do want to call attention to a body of work which considers television's representations of the domestic and builds upon the interplay between the television setting *and* the television text.

In Lynn Spigel's work on early American family sitcoms, such as *The Burns and Allen Show* (CBS, 1950–8) and *I Love Lucy* (CBS, 1951–7), and their self-reflexive representations of domesticity, she situates these programmes within the public discourses on the relationship between television, the home and the family that accompanied television's arrival in domestic space. Like the distorted reflection of the black mirror, these programmes, according to Spigel, did not present a mimetic representation of the audience's home life, but acted as a continuation of the spatial arrangement of the television within a 'home theater', presenting the home as 'a theatrical stage and thus depict[ing] highly abstract versions of family identity' (1992a, p. 19). Within other genres of television, the relationship between text and context is imaginatively explored, for example, in the work of Iris Kleinecke-Bates on domestic detail in *The Forsyte Saga* (BBC2, 1967; ITV, 2002) and Helen Wheatley on Gothic television. In reference to Susan Stewart's conceptualisation of the dollhouse, Kleinecke-Bates writes that 'watching period drama on television is an exercise in interiority: Viewed in the privacy of the own home is a miniature of another home' (2006, p. 155). Wheatley's analysis is framed by the understanding of the self-referential connection between the text and reception context of Gothic television, where the viewer is 'constantly reminded that this is terror/horror television which takes place, and is viewed, within a domestic milieu' (2006, p. 7).

Arguably, this representational relationship between text and context becomes a marker of the televisual and is evoked in accounts of television's medium specificity. Here the characteristics of domestic viewing, closeness and intimacy are explored in relation to the television image, for example, in Glen Creeber's analysis of serial drama (2004) or Alexia Smit's discussion of plastic surgery television (2010). This is work in which reflection and self-reflexivity is a founding concept.

Jane Root, co-founder of independent production company Wall to Wall and former controller of BBC Two, has written that 'television's forte is in the minutiae of human relationships, the ups and downs of domestic life. In particular, it is skilled at reflecting the detail of our everyday life back at us' (Root 1990, p. 47). *The Royle Family*, written by and starring Craig Cash and Caroline Aherne, is seemingly a perfect example of Root's argument. The critically acclaimed and much-loved series broke the conventions of British situation comedy in the late 1990s. Set in a Manchester living room, the mundane reality of this ordinary working-class family was captured by the observational style of the comedy. The action rarely left the space of the living room, though it occasionally ventured to the kitchen, and at the heart of the family was the television.[9] The dynamics of this family's life, including its gendered and generational networks of power, were played out in the space of viewing; where youngest son Anthony Ralf Little was always forced to make the tea and father Jim Ricky Tomlinson battled with Nana Liz Smith for the remote control. One might argue that a central concern of the series was the relationship between family and television,[10] and this is revealed in the opening title sequence that remained unchanged across the three original series and the now four special episodes. The sequence begins with the switching on of the television as the flash of electricity conjures up the image of Jim Royle as he heads back to his armchair. The rest of the family is introduced through a series of their television viewing moments;

Jim and Anthony erupt into laughter at what they're watching, Denise (Caroline Aherne) and Barbara (Sue Johnston) smoke and flick through a catalogue. The family is viewed from a vantage point inside the television, with the cold blue filter and flickering reception signalling the boundary of the screen. What the sequence sets up is a complex series of reflections, where both the viewer and the Royles look into and out from the television screen; the final image of the sequence constructing a portrait of a family frozen in the twilight of the screen's reflection, lost in its magnetic pull (see Figure 1.3).

This play with subject positions illuminates the programme's forms of televisual identification and engagement. Arguably, it was in its audience's identification with the everydayness of the Royles and the role of television viewing that the programme found its biggest draw. *The Royle Family* managed to situate television not just as part of daily life but as part of a system of everyday memory-making; the family's squabbles, laughter, banalities, celebrations and tragedies all caught in the act of viewing.

On its return in 2006 for the broadcast of the special episode 'The Royle Family: The Queen of Sheba', Stuart Maconie wrote in the *Radio Times* that 'this is their [Aherne and Cash's] childhood on screen – for many of us *our* childhood. So much so that, as Peter Kay has remarked, you thought they must have tapes of your own family evenings' (2006,

Figure 1.3   Television's mise-en-abyme – a series of reflections looking into and out from the screen. *The Royle Family* title sequence (Granada for BBC, 1998–).

p. 18). The series evoked for many the memory of their own family dynamics and viewing practices, but the 2006 special also brought with it the memory of viewing the original series. The British televisual land-scape had changed for all, including the Royles; the family now watches on a giant plasma screen and Denise's tale of Sky+ viewing is met with wide eyes and wonder. Despite these new technologies and prac-tices, television is for the Royles, as Helen Wood and Lisa Taylor have argued in opposition to the technologically deterministic accounts of new media, as 'durably and consistently located in the fabric of every-day life as it ever was' (2008, p. 14). The family's constant and discordant chirping of the theme music to the BBC's early evening magazine pro-gramme *The One Show* (2006–) in the episode 'The Golden Egg cup' represents the affectionate hold that television still has on the family.

The Royle Family has also always been about change and transition, with the constancy of family and television anchoring its members. Whilst some things change, others remain the same, and each time we still return to the preserved portrait of the family in the title sequence. The curve of the pre-LCD glass television screen, represented by the fade to black at the edge of the image, and the flickering of analogue recep-tion evokes a sense of 'pastness'. The reflection here becomes a looking back, not only at the way we were, but also at the way we once watched.

Home from home: *Family History*

A simulated home from home is employed across a variety of television programmes and genres; from the 'fully rounded sensual experience' (Lury 2005, p. 161) of the Royle's family home to the Ikea-furnished sets of daytime television studios. It is this relationship between television's representations of the domestic and its setting within the domestic that is explored in Gillian Wearing's 2006 installation *Family History*.[11]

Writing on the work of Nam June Paik and Wolf Vostell, artists working in the context of 1960s America, John G. Hanhardt argues that their work offers a 'profound insight into television, not as a found object to be recontextualised as art, but as an icon to be bro-ken of its authority' (1990, p. 113). These artists provide early examples of the attempt to decontextualise and defamiliarise the television set whilst offering a commentary on and critique of commercial televi-sion. Following Hanhardt, David Morley considers how these works of deconstruction provide the academic with a way of viewing television differently (2007, p. 282) – an alternative way, like the black mirror, of 'estranging perception'.

Family History might be seen to sit in relation to this early work. It is similarly involved in defamiliarising television but it does this by investigating an autobiographical connection to television through the artist's memories of the pioneering 1970s reality television series *The Family* (BBC, 1974).[12] *Family History* is a multi-layered and ambitious project that continues Wearing's interest in reality television and confessional cultures (exhibited in celebrated works such as *Confess All On Video. Don't Worry, You Will Be In Disguise. Intrigued? Call Gillian...* (1994)) and a preoccupation with family and history (see her photographic series *Album* (2003) in which Wearing recreates photos/portraits of six family members with Wearing posing, using detailed prosthetic masks, in place of each relative).

Rather than being exhibited in a traditional gallery space, *Family History* was installed in two 'show homes' in Reading and Birmingham; the significance of the locations part of the piece itself and its 'revisiting' of its own 'points of origin' (Bode, Walwin and Watkins, 2007). Wearing grew up in 1970s Birmingham and *The Family* featured the Wilkins family of Reading. The show home setting is also chosen as a deliberate contrast with the 1970s milieu of the Wearing's living room and the Wilkins' home. The cold (literally) and antiseptic spaces of the show home – neutral palettes and minimalist design – draw the audience's attention to the change in ideas of home and domestic design; from the cluttered and colourful suburban homes of the Wearings and the Wilkins to the aspirational living of the city-centre apartment.

The installation itself features two screens in different rooms in the empty apartment. In the first room, on a small LCD screen hung at eye level on the wall, is the film of a young girl with long dark brown hair and wearing a red 1970s dress, watching an episode of *The Family*. The girl is a stand-in for the adult Wearing. She is dressed in a replica of the artist's childhood clothes and is watching television in a detailed mock-up of the artist's old family living room. With a toy truck, a glass bowl and two photographs of Wearing and her sister arranged on the 1970s wood-panelled television set, a bowl of fruit and an ashtray sitting on top of a nest of tables in front of glossy salmon pink curtains, the 'authenticity' of the replica room and costume is verified by original Wearing family photographs published in the project book. Back to the screen, we see the girl absorbed in her viewing of *The Family*, then later she turns to the camera to offer her own thoughts on the programme.

On the second, much larger, screen is a long interview with Heather Wilkins, teenage member of the Wilkins family, now grown up with children of her own. In a brightly lit television studio she is interviewed by veteran talk show host Trisha Goddard. The interview is conventional in style, with the professional Goddard and a much more media-savvy Heather. She talks about her experience of filming *The Family*, the public reception of the series and her life after it, and the interview is intercut with scenes from the original series to which Heather is also prompted to look back and respond.

At the end of the interview Wearing orchestrates her own 'reveal'. The camera pulls back from the comfy television studio to reveal not only the 'constructedness' of the set, the lighting rig and flimsy MDF walls, but also that, in fact, the installation's two components, its two living rooms, are built side-by-side. The revelation of this proximity is much more than a Brechtian stunt and works to illuminate, to make visible, television's dynamics of closeness and intimacy.

In the accompanying book to the installation Steven Bode, of the Film and Video Umbrella, writes of Wearing's project as:

> a portrait of one child of television by another; a woman who, to a significant extent grew up on television rendered, affectionately and acutely, by an artist who grew up with television. Blending biography and autobiography, it is a piece that uses the language of television, not in a spirit of appropriation or the service of reconstruction or deconstruction, but as a shared vernacular language with which both artist and subject are familiar; a language, indeed, with which we are all familiar; a language which, even more now than in the 1970s, is real to us – a language of the everyday.
>
> (2007)

The 'language' of reality television and the talk show are the televisual forms that Wearing predominantly employs within her piece, and in particular, it offers a commentary on and responds to the artist's own fascination with reality television (the discussion of which is central to the interviews Wearing conducted as publicity for the installation). But it is how *memories* of television emerge as a 'shared venacular language' and a 'language of the everyday' that is of interest here. The revealed structure of the set, like the title sequence of *The Royle Family*, highlights a pattern of reflections; through the simulated past/present of the adjoining 'sets', one a reconstruction and the other a retrospective, the project interrogates the making of memory within television's various living rooms.

Whilst the cultural historical work of Lynn Spigel and Tim O'Sullivan examines the post-war arrival of television in the home as a technological novelty and a signifier of modernity, later generations, like Wearing's, have grown up with television. For the child of analogue television, television was a familiar object and a regulator of daily life. These generational differences in attitudes towards television are extremely significant and largely unexplored (though Karen Lury's study *British Youth Television* (2001) is a welcome and evocative exception). We must also remain alert to the presence of the television programme-maker, critic and academic within these generational audiences.

Growing up with television: *Freaks and Geeks*

There is a moment early on in the episode 'Dead Dogs and Gym Teachers' in the celebrated American teen series *Freaks and Geeks*, where, after a humiliating experience in gym class, Bill Haverchuck (Martin Starr), the loveable, lanky and bespectacled geek, returns home, makes himself a grilled-cheese sandwich and sits down in front of the television. Framed by and scored to the non-diegetic soundtrack of 'I'm One' by The Who, we watch Bill watching Garry Shandling tell jokes on Dinah Shore's talk show (*Dinah!* CBS, 1974–80) in what feels like an intensely private and intimate scene. The sequence, cut in time to the music and building across the chorus, cuts back and forth between Bill and the television image, progressively pulling closer to both the image of Bill in fits of laughter and the analogue-quality image of Shandling smiling back. A sense of the character's interaction with the television is created by this movement to close-up and the mirroring of the shots – as Garry raises his glass to the studio audience, Bill raises his glass of milk to Garry (see Figure 1.4).

The sequence is evocative of the character's private relationship with television as part of an after-school routine. Where television is the cruel mistress in *Oldboy*, in *Freaks and Geeks* the relationship is a warm camaraderie, a safe and comforting place away from the hostilities of growing up. In a touching movement within Starr's performance he signals his closeness and identification with Garry by subtly gesturing with his hands towards the screen then back at himself as if to say 'me too!'

Framed within a series about the trials of adolescence, the role of television within a body of cultural references which bond the friendships of the characters (the freaks bond primarily through music, the geeks through film, television and comedy) is highlighted. Whilst the references are generationally specific, the experience of their use within everyday life and conversation is arguably cross-generational. The sequence operates nostalgically as part of the programme-makers'

Figure 1.4   Garry Shandling and Bill Haverchuck share an after-school drink in 'Dead Dogs and Gym Teachers', episode 14, *Freaks and Geeks* (dir. Judd Apatow, prod. Apatow Productions/DreamWorks SKG, 1999).

memory of television; the series is set in a high school in the suburbs of Detroit in the early 1980s and is based on the teenage experiences of the writers, the show's creator, Paul Feig, and co-producer, Judd Apatow. In an interview, Apatow refers to this sequence, commenting that 'that's what I did every afternoon for years when I was a kid' (in Goodwin 2007), and the intimacy of the moment is arguably reflective of the recognition of Bill's relationship with television as a potentially shared experience. What is primarily of interest within this moment is the representation of an experience of television and how that is filtered through the lens of memory. It is a memory of living with and growing up with television, the memory of a routine and a ritual as much as it is a memory of Garry Shandling telling jokes on TV.

Seasons, light, memory and magic

Writing on the BBC's embeddedness within twentieth-century British society and culture, David Cardiff and Paddy Scannell argue that 'nothing so well illustrates the unobtrusive way in which the BBC came to establish itself as an agent of the national culture as [the] calendrical role of broadcasting, [the] cyclical reproduction, year in, year out, of an orderly and regular progression of festivities, rituals and celebrations which marked out the unfolding of the year' (Cardiff and Scannell 1987, p. 160). The broadcast of such events 'are marked up not only on the public calendar of "history" but also on the private calendar of people's lives' (Scannell 1996, p. 91). Commemorations and anniversaries are key rituals within the unfolding of the year and the calendar is arguably a determining factor in the commissioning and production of, to quote Tobias Ebbrecht, 'historical event television' (2007a, 2007b). However, attempting to move away from the dominance of media events within the understandings of television memories, it is the 'private calendar of people's lives' which interests me here. What I want to think through is how the unfolding and dynamic processes of television within the context of everyday, domestic space allow for a different and additional conceptualisation of television memories.

In Jerome Bourdon's study of audience memories of television in France he describes the category of 'wallpaper memories' as memories of habits and routines.[13] Whilst a useful categorisation, the significance of the television in both the construction of the routine and the memory of it is somewhat elided by the idea of the medium as simply providing 'wallpaper' to the remembered scene. For me, for my memories, television is an integral part of that scene and a network of senses and impressions that constitute an experience of living within domestic space and within a particular society. Television, for me, is remembered as a sensual experience, and in particular is characterised by the memories of light. It is television's complex and powerful relationship between interior and exterior, and the layering of forms and patterns of light, that we might use to characterise the formation of memory within this sensual experience.

The varied arrangements of light in the space of viewing, both natural and artificial, in some senses become emblematic of the different forms of engagement on offer by different forms of television. The closing of curtains and the turning out of lights might be seen as attempts to recreate the conditions of cinema viewing at home in order to view films or to concentrate on the narrative demands of a series such as *The Wire* (HBO, 2002–8) or the spectacle of natural history in *Planet Earth* (BBC, 2006). Though perhaps clichéd, these conditions of viewing are evocative of forms of engagement. Ellis' early notion of glance theory (1982) is based upon the condition of viewing among the hustle and bustle of daily domestic life and work. The conditions of viewing also produce sensual environments and moods in which memories of television are framed. The sense of indulgence and guilt of watching television inside on a sunny day, with the windows open, the curtains closed and the sounds of summer competing with the programme, the annoyance of shafts of light falling on the screen via ill-fitting curtains; viewing on dark nights with the curtains open, the heating on and condensation misting up the windows, drawing attention to the cold outside. These are environments from which my own memories are drawn. I recall as a child lying in front of the television on a deep-pile green carpet watching music videos. I remember the warmth I felt from a patch of sunshine falling through the patio windows correlating with the song I was seeing and hearing (a-ha's 'The Sun Always Shines on TV'). Early evening in winter, the dark outside, the misted windows, still wearing a crumpled school uniform and the fantastical sounds and colours of *Star Trek* (NBC, 1966–9), broadcast at teatime on BBC Two, radiating throughout the room. These are not memories of the detail of the programmes (though I've seen the music video many times since, I've never really watched *Star Trek*), neither are they purely memories of the context, but they are an interplay between the two and the sense impressions left by the play of light, texture, colour, sound and temperature. As memories they are not fully formed; they are fragments, not the 'flashbulbs' seen to characterise the experience of viewing media events but more like the flickers of the old analogue signal. These 'flickers' are not momentous, life-changing or memorialised (though they are undeniably tinged with nostalgia) but they are both informed by and provide a sense of the experiences and memories of viewing throughout the year and the changing pattern of seasons and light which provide both ever-changing and routine environments of viewing.[14]

The domestic environment, though certainly not unique in this characteristic, can produce a system and layering of space and reflection, both inside and out, in which the television screen is incorporated. These are most apparent at night. On a dark evening the domestic scene can be bounced back by the windows, layering the inside onto the night outside. From the outside, travelling through suburban areas on journeys to and from home, television sets appear as luminous squares of light beaming out from a parade of homes, and when viewed from a bus or car window are layered behind the reflections of the self inside the vehicle.[15] These layers of reflection and vision call attention to the relationship between the home and the world outside, but they don't necessarily produce a binary division between the two, where the home offers safety and shelter from a threatening and hostile world. Instead they illuminate a long history of ambivalence in relation to this dynamic, where forms of alienation, fear and anxiety infiltrate and are exposed.

Behind the mirror: closeness and distance

In Douglas Sirk's family melodrama *All That Heaven Allows* (1955), Cary (Jane Wyman) gives up her lover and gardener Ron (Rock Hudson) for the sake of her children, though when her children subsequently announce they are moving on themselves, so as not to leave their mother alone, they offer her the gift of a television set (though she has previously refused to get one). The set appears as an enforced and meagre substitute for the companionship of both Ron and her children and the enthusiastic patter of the salesman is made ironic by the representation of the set.

> All you have to do is turn that dial and you have all the company you want, right there on the screen. Drama, comedy, life's parade at your fingertips.

This promotional promise is undermined by a mournful score and the slow zoom into the television screen that frames Cary's anxious and melancholy reflection. Her hands clasped together and brow knotted, with a sense of horror she stares back at herself imprisoned in the screen (see Figure 1.5). As opposed to the excessive colour of Sirk's melodrama and the bright-red ribbon which adorns the set, within the borders of the television screen, a frame within a (cinema) frame, the image remains sharp but the palette is muted and drained. Made strange and estranging by the effect of the screen as a black mirror, the image reflected is haunting and uncanny. A warning from film on the dangers

Figure 1.5 Imprisoned by television. Jane Wyman in *All That Heaven Allows* (dir. Douglas Sirk, prod. Universal, US, 1955).

of television, the new medium, in this instance, traps its viewer in a ghostly existence.

Where the etymology of nostalgia draws us to the significance of the home, so does an understanding of the uncanny. From the German 'unheimlich', translated as 'unhomely', Freud describes the uncanny as 'that class of the frightening which leads back to what is known of old and long familiar' (1990 (1919), p. 340). The concept highlights a series of additional responses to television's place in a domestic environment. It is evocative of the potential threat posed by the merging of the private and the public, interior and exterior, and expressive of a dynamic of closeness and distance, which includes the recognition of, and estrangement from, the self.

The work of Jeffrey Sconce explores the uncanny rendering of domestic space by considering television as a 'haunted apparatus'. He observes that – 'there remains the disturbing thought that, just as we can potentially peer into other worlds through the television, these other worlds may be peering back into our own living room' (2000, p. 144). What emerges across his work is not only the potential intrusions brought into the home by the television signal but also a notion of the television screen as a magic surface and a conduit between worlds – private and public, the home and the supernatural. To return to and continue the alignment between television and the 'black mirror', this imagining of television is suggestive of the potential space *behind* the mirror and recalls the 'terror aroused by the black mirror [...] for if one calls on the demons often enough, they are sure to come' (Maillet, 2004, p. 51). In the Japanese horror film *Ringu* (dir. Hideo Nakata, Japan, 1998), remade as *The Ring* (dir. Gore Verbinski, US, 2002), the television, following such films and programmes as *Poltergeist* (dir. Tobe Hooper, US, 1982) and *Ghostwatch* (BBC, 1992), is once again the site of horror. The fear of invasion is materialised in the unnatural movement of the vengeful spirit of Sadako/Samara, from the grainy and flickering video image and through the screen to inflict a terrifying death upon the haunted viewer of a cursed VHS tape (see Figure 1.6).

Clearly offering a self-reflexive form of terror, television and video technology and its intimate place within the domestic setting, the home and the family are played upon by horror fiction, but it is a playfulness that doesn't lose sight of these spaces as potential *sites* of violence and trauma as well as *receivers* of images of violence and trauma. Whilst an analysis of this would take me down a different line of inquiry, the notion of the domestic as a haunted space, one which reverberates with loss, longing and the potentially more benign phantoms of absent family and friends, is explored in more detail in the following chapter

Figure 1.6   Television as the site of horror and haunting: *Ringu* (dir. Hideo Nakata, Japan, 1998).

and in relation to the patterns of reflection and return within television drama. The reverberations of memory, imagined here as a form of haunting, allow us to rethink television as part of an everyday system of memory-making and, by paying attention to the set and the screen, television emerges not as a postmodern icon of an 'electronic nowhere' (Sconce 2000, p. 17), but remembered and experienced as both living and lived with.

The television altar

In Ondina Fachel Leal's discussion of the place and space of television within the Brazilian home she offers an analysis of the television *entourage* or altar on display in one particular domestic arrangement. Here the items of the entourage, including plastic flowers, a religious picture, a false gold vase and family photographs, act as 'interconnected pieces of one coherent set' (1990, p. 21); a symbolic system which reveals dimensions of class, taste and identity. The symbolic power of the television set anchors the display – it is an object of pride and cultural capital, positioned to be visible from the street. Leal argues that 'the TV object here is a fetish in the sense that it is infused with an ethereal magical meaning [...] even when it is turned off and when no one is watching it' (1990, p. 24). I want to conclude with two moments from two of the programmes analysed in this book. They are examples that offer a vision of the television altar in two television homes and which reveal aspects of both its symbolic power and its memorial function.

In the opening of David Baddiel's episode from the first series of *Who Do You Think You Are?*,[16] the comedian, inviting the cameras into his home, introduces the producer/audience to two pictures of his maternal grandfather, Ernst Fabian. The first is an image of Baddiel and his brothers as schoolboys being read a story by their grandfather. The second is of Ernst and his wife Otti, a 'happy' image taken in the early 1930s before Baddiel's Jewish grandparents fled from Germany in 1939. They are both framed photographs which sit upon the marble mantelpiece in the centre of the living room and are 2 images within a display of approximately 11 framed family photos. Hung on the wall, just above the mantle, is a small flat-screen television (see Figure 1.7).

This arrangement of domestic space and personal objects, including the television set, is not entirely unfamiliar. In many cases the television sits among or even provides a mantelpiece for photographs and mementos (in my home it sits among driftwood collected with my father, a small plastic penguin belonging to my nephew and a framed

Figure 1.7   David Baddiel's television altar (*WDYTYA*, series 1, episode 7, Wall to Wall for BBC, 2004).

photobooth image of myself and my sister). This can also be extended to the digital interfaces of multiplatform viewing, where the window of the iPlayer, for example, sits upon or is juxtaposed against digital albums and desktop photographs. In Baddiel's home, the television is part of a network of images and a spatial arrangement covered with personal history and memory. These two images commence the investigative trail and establish Baddiel's 'strong emotional connection' to the memory of his grandfather, and the use of the family archive operates as a point of access for the viewers, interjecting them into the practices of history and memory-making explored in the family history documentary. But the scene also testifies to the domestic and intimate nature of television's setting within the home and reveals potential consequences for the viewing experience of television programmes about personal history and memory viewed within a domestic memory network.

To return to *The Royle Family*, both this interplay and the significance of the television as altar are illuminated in the 2006 special episode 'The Queen of Sheba'. At the wake following the death of Nana, the urn containing her ashes is put – 'pride of place in the Royle Family household'. As Jim Royle places the urn 'somewhere where we'll *always* be reminded of her' – on top of the television – the family bursts into rapturous applause (see Figure 1.8). Nana is accompanied by the ashes of neighbour Mary (Doreen Keogh) in the 2010 Christmas special 'Joe's Crackers' and in a short montage sequence of Christmas family snaps,

Figure 1.8 Nana takes pride of place on the Royle Family's television altar. 'The Queen of Sheba' (dir. Mark Mylod, prod. Granada for BBC, 2006).

the family and their loved ones have their pictures taken in front of the television and in various poses with Nana and Mary. For the Royles and for many of us, the television forms part of a material network of memory; it is both a reminder of, and a member of, the family.

2
Haunting the Memory: Moments of Return in Television Drama

'Everything. Everyone. Everywhere. Ends' was the tag line for the fifth and final season of the critically acclaimed series *Six Feet Under* (HBO, 2001–5) – a dark comic drama centred on the lives of the Fisher family and their family-run funeral home in Los Angeles. In the final episode ('Everyone's Waiting', season 5, episode 12), following the death of her oldest brother Nate (Peter Krause), the youngest sibling Claire (Lauren Ambrose) leaves the family and Los Angeles. With no job lined up but an ambition to become a photographer, she pulls away from the family home and drives into an uncertain future. What follows is a remarkable six-minute sequence, framed by the track 'Breathe' by the female singer-songwriter Sia, in which Claire literally drives into that future. The sequence intercuts shots of Claire driving, the back projection speeded up to heighten the 'fantastical' feel of the scene, with a montage of the weddings, celebrations, deaths and funerals in the remaining lives of the Fisher family – a six-minute sequence which spans 80 years.[1] Here the future is foretold but its possibilities are asserted by the long road disappearing into the horizon, where the series ends and where we leave Claire driving.

The sequence is both an ending and a beginning. Whilst there is the space for the viewer to imagine the drama in between, the character's storylines are taken to their final moments. There is an insistence on the inevitability of the ending but the cyclical patterns of life are also reaffirmed. To quote Umberto Eco's thoughts on serial narratives – 'what becomes celebrated here is a sort of victory of life over art, with the paradoxical result that the era of electronics, instead of emphasizing the phenomena of shock, interruption, novelty, and frustration of expectations, would produce a return to the continuum, the Cyclical, the Periodical, the Regular' (1990, p. 96).

Six Feet Under reverses the logic of the 'reflective coda', projecting forward rather than reflecting back. This is not to argue that the final montage insists upon a forward momentum; it also sets up a pattern of return well established throughout the series via a succession of 'hauntings'. The members of the Fisher family, and Nate in particular, are regularly 'haunted' by their father, killed in the pilot episode after a collision with a bus. At the opening of the coda it is the 'ghost' of her brother Nate that motivates Claire to go when she wants to stay, and as she pulls away from the family home she glances in the wing mirror of her car. Framed in the mirror is the image of Nate, jogging behind the car (see Figure 2.1). Overlapping briefly, the two lines of vision and movement inevitably separate and the image slowly drops out of the reflection as the car speeds up and travels on. It is this moment that haunts me. Whilst it returns us to the familiar image of Nate running, it returns us only to a reflection that poignantly drops out of view. The return is accompanied by a retreat, capturing a pattern of haunting and a recharged sense of loss.

Writing on what he perceives to be the ghostly movement of narrative, Julian Wolfreys argues that 'the movement of the return is not simply that, for that which is spectral is only ever perceived indirectly by the traces it has left. It has in returning, already begun to retreat' (2002, p. 3). For me, this captures a wider characteristic of

Figure 2.1   Six Feet Under, 'Everyone's Waiting', season 5, episode 12 (dir. Alan Ball, prod. HBO/The Greenblatt Janollari Studio/Actual Size Productions, US, 2005).

television understood as an 'ebb and flow'. It is a characteristic that I want to explore further in relation to the representations of remembering and reflection in television drama and to offer some thoughts on the function of memory in the narrative design of serial drama. It is these moments of return that I am particularly interested in, specifically their self-conscious play with ideas of haunting, the resonance of 'afterimages' and the forms, functions and pleasures of repetition.

The moment can be momentary, fleeting, an instant in the movement of time. The moment can also be momentous, have moving power and be of consequence or importance.[2] Within the term itself there is a strange tension between movement and stasis. These 'moments' should also be considered in relation to the understandings of television as a sequential medium and its characteristics of flow and segmentation; television as, to quote Richard Dyer, the 'apotheosis of seriality' (2000, p. 146) and its characteristics of flow and regularity or repetition. As Stephen Heath and Gillian Skirrow argued in 1977:

> The central fact of television experience is much less flow than flow and regularity; the anachronistic succession is also a constant repetition and these terms of *movement and stasis* can be found as well within the single programme as within the evening's viewing.
>
> (My emphasis, 1977, p. 15)

The rhythm of movement and stasis, the cyclicality and endlessness of the television text, emerges most clearly in writing on the soap opera (see, for example, Geraghty 1981), and recurs again in recent work on 'quality' serial television drama. Heath and Skirrow's argument correlates with Michael Newman's work on the structure of storytelling in the prime-time serial and his analysis of the 'beats' and 'arcs', the story structures and patterns dictated by production contexts and commercial imperatives that run across scenes, episodes and seasons (2006).

Considering these part/whole relations and looking at the patterns and repetitions that are visible in serial drama reveals some of their central pleasures. They also work to generate forms of resonance, associative possibilities and allusive meanings that can reveal the significance of thinking through the relationship between television and memory. Central to this relationship is the idea of the television viewing experience as one of accumulation, where viewing experiences and references are built up over time, and the memory of 'afterimages' and 'moments' is accumulated over a life lived across television.

In Frank Kermode's *The Sense of an Ending* (1967), a historical and philosophical discussion of 'endings' in literature, he quotes the poem 'Reference Back' by Philip Larkin:

> Truly, though our element is time,
> We are not suited to the long perspectives
> Open at each instant of our lives.
> They link us to our losses:

Television has the potential to offer this 'long perspective' and the ways in which it references back are complex and varied and are investigated across this book. Remembering and reflection become central to television's defining characteristic of repetition. 'Adorno's reproach' is often invoked to critique this characteristic (see Caughie 1991) – one which is also at the heart of the discourses of trauma and therapy that circulate in relation to both television and memory studies. Here, television's 'compulsion to repeat', its performance of a 'ghost dance of the undead', generates a psychoanalytic resonance for many commentators (Elsaesser 1999). Within television's serial forms, though, this 'compulsion to repeat effectively becomes a fundamental principle of narrative construction' informed by a commercial imperative (Davies 2007, p. 28).

Matt Hills' work on the construction of moments in the new *Doctor Who* (BBC, 2005–) opens up some additional lines of inquiry into the idea of the 'moment', particularly in the way in which moments within the series are constructed to be 'memorable' but also in the way they increase the dispersibility of the text – moments which can be extracted for publicity materials (2008). The idea of the 'memorable moment' is central for forms of nostalgia programming and the repackaging and repurposing of the text – which I shall return to in Chapter 4 – but they are often 'memorable moments' in that they are moments of or about memory. This is certainly the case in relation to the programmes I have chosen to discuss in this chapter on television drama.

My first example is *Perfect Strangers* (BBC, 2001), a three-part drama by the high-profile British writer and director Stephen Poliakoff. Described as 'a laureate of memory' (Freedland 2004) much of Poliakoff's work, within the last ten years at least, has been preoccupied with the themes of history, memory and nostalgia. Within the context of this chapter his work opens up a discussion of the ways in which memory and remembering are represented by television's dramatic forms. Though *Perfect Strangers* is only a three-part series, paying attention to its own moments of repetition and return reveals much about how allusive meanings and serial patterns can be generated. Here I will shift my attention to consider the longer forms of serial drama, in this case, three contemporary and high-profile American shows – *ER*, *Grey's Anatomy* and *The Wire*. Faced with a familiar problem for the television scholar of thinking and writing about serial television, with approximately 400 hours of drama to consider, the very length of the programmes can lead to a series of observations about time and memory. The study of 'moments' allows a way of approaching the breadth and complexity of the material, and to define the object of study further, I want to think specifically about endings and beginnings as privileged spaces for reflection and remembering, where patterns are initiated and revealed.

Beyond the 'endlessness' of the soap opera (see Geraghty 1981 and Allen 1985) or the 'non-ending' of *The Sopranos* (HBO, 1999–2007) (see Polan 2009) there has been little discussion of endings in television drama or across television's many generic forms. Endings or 'milestone moments' often function as reflective and self-reflexive spaces within serial drama that 'reference back' on their own long perspectives. The cumulative narratives of serial drama demand and reward certain levels of audience investment in character and diegesis, often over hundreds of hours of programming. For Jonathan Gray television is an 'expansive art' that has the 'power to tell enduring, deeply involving, and complex stories over significant time' (2008, p. 27). Whilst memory in these examples might be viewed as a basic imperative of televisual forms of storytelling, where 'previously on' sequences operate as an aide-memoire, its significance is explicitly revealed through reflective moments, often occurring in anniversary episodes or moments of character/narrative upheaval or closure.[3]

The endings of television's serial forms, from *ER* and *The Wire* to sitcoms such as *Friends* (NBC, 1994–2004) and *Frasier* (NBC, 1993–2004), are often produced to generate specific feelings of finality (though the premature or unmarked endings of cancelled series will offer different forms of resonance). They reflect upon the life of the series but also invite the viewer to reflect upon their own investment in that series. This is clearly exemplified by Frasier's final words on KACL radio, where the distinction between character and actor (Kelsey Grammer), fictional radio and real television audience collapses within the performance, marking the 'end of an era' – 'I have loved every minute with my KACL family and all of you. For 11 years you've heard me say "I'm listening", well you were listening too – and for that I'm eternally grateful. Goodnight Seattle.'

These reflective moments are not unique to serial drama and are organised by a series of genres and forms, from the concluding reflective montages at the end of major news and sporting events, to the 'best bits' of departing contestants in reality entertainment formats such as *Big Brother* (Channel 4, 2000–10) and *The X Factor* (ITV, 2004–). Kermode writes that 'when we survive, we make little images of moments which have seemed like ends' (1967, p. 7), and these montages similarly operate as textual processes of marking and memorialising. Within serial drama, in such instances, memories of television are written into serial narratives through practices of self-citation and self-referentiality. Operating as a reflective device for character, narrative and audience, these moments in the life of a programme reveal how television *is* meaningful in many instances because of the way that it interacts with memory. Such instances can illuminate the qualities of serial television but also provide a commentary on the comparative function of television memory and nostalgia.

The purpose of this chapter is neither to retrieve a sense of 'monumentality' (Caughie 2000, p. 13) nor to argue directly for the place of the examples I discuss within a canon of great moments, episodes or shows, but to investigate some of the ways in which memory, perhaps more specifically remembering, is represented within some of television's dramatic forms and how a focus on memory might reveal more about the ways in which television works. Memory has also emerged as a key narrative and thematic concern across the history of television drama and points towards the central role of television in the construction of cultural memories, identities and histories. Historic, national and generic contexts inevitably influence the different stories being told and the different ways in which memory is employed and represented. Within a history of British television drama, for example, from Dennis Potter's *Blue Remembered Hills* (BBC1, 1979) and *The Singing Detective* (BBC1, 1986) to recent successes *Life on Mars* and *Ashes to Ashes* (BBC1, 2008–10), the creative, imaginative and comparative ways in which memory and nostalgia are evoked through dramatic forms would provide the scope for further research and analysis.

This might take the form of considering the work of specific dramatists. Stephen Poliakoff's work has a clear authorial style (see Nelson 2006). Privileged with an unusual level of creative control, Poliakoff is often perceived as a rarity, a leftover from an earlier age of British television drama. I will return to the nostalgic figure of Poliakoff in my discussion of 'Golden Ages' in Chapter 4. However, I have decided not to frame my analysis in this chapter through the work and influence of the 'author', 'creator' or even 'show runner', but to consider the stories that are told and how memory is evoked and utilised. I am interested in the hauntings of and by characters, the traces that return and retreat and the ways in which, for television drama 'to tell a story is always to invoke ghosts, to open a space through which something other returns' (Wolfreys 2002, p. 3).

Perfect Strangers (BBC, 2001)

A wealthy patriarch from a grand London family throws a three-day family reunion. From the sleepy suburbs of London, Daniel (Matthew Macfadyen), his mother Esther (Jill Baker) and his irascible father Raymond (Michael Gambon) form the 'Hillingdon contingent' of the family tree. On arriving at the luxurious hotel in the centre of London, Daniel is confronted by both glamorous and eccentric members of the family he's never met before, including Alice (Lindsay Duncan), the captivating first lady of the family; Charles (Toby Stephens) and Rebecca (Claire Skinner), the alluring and secretive brother and sister; strange and spivvy Irving (Timothy Spall) and the family's fastidious 'archive man', Stephen (Anton Lesser). As the reunion progresses over a series of functions, Daniel searches for his place in the family and all the family members are confronted by memories of the past as the secrets and stories behind the family tree are revealed.

Poliakoff asserts in interview that 'there are at least three great stories in every family'.[4] In *Perfect Strangers* there are four principal secrets that make up the narrative. Stephen's secret tells the story of his mother, a young German–Jewish girl, and her escape from the fate of the rest of her family. A Second World War story also lies behind the three elderly sisters: the eldest sister's bereavement when her fiancé is killed in battle, and from which she never recovers, and how the two younger siblings run away from home and live as feral children during the course of the war.

The other two stories are framed as mysteries that motivate the narrative across the three parts, and which prompt the anxiety and the investigations of both Daniel and Raymond. Having been presented at the reunion with unremembered but enigmatic photographs of their childhoods, they begin to search for their significance. The photographs are eventually discovered to be part of the story of Raymond's father's secret life and love affair revealed at the end of the drama – a secret which reconnects father, son and grandson. The reason behind the estrangement between Alice and Rebecca and Charles is the other driving force of the narrative. Daniel's discovery of Richard's (JJ Feild) story, the brother of Rebecca and Charles who is 'accidentally' missed off the family tree, explains the rupture between the siblings and the woman who raised them as her own. Richard's mental illness led to his exclusion from the family, and his subsequent suicide left Alice, Rebecca and Charles dealing with the complexities of their own guilt and blame. Poliakoff weaves a complex web of desire and bereavement as the siblings seduce the unknowing Daniel into taking the place of Richard, and as Daniel seeks to find his own place in the family he attempts to heal the rupture between Alice, Rebecca and Charles.

In part three, Daniel engineers a meeting between Rebecca, Charles and Alice. This final confrontation takes place in a grand summer house that sits in the grounds of the lavish country estate that once belonged to 'The family'. As Rebecca stares out of the window and across part of the gardens, from her point of view we see the three old sisters in the distance, walking down a garden path. Running behind, then overtaking them, are the three young siblings that had just previously and briefly interrupted the initial confrontation. In this one moment, three generations of the family are presented in parallel. Though the narrative remains focused on the story of Rebecca, Charles and Richard, the appearance of two other groups of siblings suggests an echo in the drama between the different family stories and secrets. This echo is further emphasised by the sound of the children's laughter as they run off to play hide and seek, recalling the footage of the young Rebecca, Charles and Richard enjoying similar childhood games. In this moment a sense of the conflation of the past, present and future is evoked. Though the content of the stories remains deeply personal and individual there is the sense of a shared experience and the patterns that emerge in the family. The tales of sibling love and parental rejection are emphasised.

The echoes and repetitions that exist at the level of both the narrative and the image in *Perfect Strangers* are intricate and numerous. Sarah Cardwell's (2005) excellent close textual analysis of the sequence that reveals the mystery behind the photographs of Daniel dressed as the little prince and of Raymond's father dancing identifies the repetitions and patternings that dominate the drama and analyses how they are elaborately woven into the text. Whilst Cardwell's analysis is bound to the sequence in question, the above moment illuminates the significance of those echoes for the design of the narrative and the construction of the characters that make up the family – a design which relies upon the cyclicality of generational memory and sets up a system of generational replacement that is in evidence in the other examples discussed within this chapter. Echoes and repetitions also feature throughout the drama via the repeated irruption of images into the text and the recurring flashes of character memory – moments which evoke an experience of remembering.

Remembering Richard

Writing on the flashback in film, Maureen Turim argues that 'flashbacks often present images which are to be understood as memories. These films portray their own versions of how memories are stored, how they are repressed, how they return from the repressed [...] flashback films make specific use of the theory of associative memory, the way an event or sensation in the present brings forth a memory trace that was since forgotten' (1989, p. 19). Turim's argument would seem to correlate with Pam Cook's discussion of the nostalgia film and how the elisions between past and present might be seen to 'reflect the activity of memory itself' (2005, p. 16). In *Perfect Strangers* the devices of irruption and repetition begin to characterise that activity. The characteristic of irruption refers to those flashes of memory that appear to us – those sense impressions that pull us out of time and back to a former version of ourselves – and recalls Proust's conception of *mémoire involontaire*, where he is transported back to the past via the taste of a madeleine.[5] There is one particular moment in Alice's telling of Richard's story, in part three of the drama, where this characteristic of irruption is skilfully articulated.

Alice and Daniel sit opposite one another at a small kitchen table in Alice's London apartment. The positioning of the characters recalls Lindsay Duncan's performance as the storyteller in *Shooting the Past* (BBC, 1999), though this time her character is telling the story from her own memory and experience. Alice's narration is accompanied by both the narrative reconstruction of the events surrounding Richard's illness and the use of photographic montages, such as a series of black-and-white and colour photographs that depict the troubled Richard, cloaked in his black leather coat, walking barefoot through the streets of London like a poet or flâneur left over from a previous era. However, the story is also littered with inconsequential detail – images of Richard that do not immediately correspond with Alice's narration, which irrupt into the frame as they flicker across the memory. The collage of images that is seemingly extracted from Alice's memory builds up an impression of her private history, but also gives us a sense of Richard's own character filtered through Alice's memory, the fragmented and sporadic nature of which begins to reflect the characterisation of a young man falling

Figure 2.2   Alice, present (*Perfect Strangers*, dir. Stephen Poliakoff, prod. Talkback for BBC, 2001).

apart. Through the collage of stories and images, memories and reconstructions, Poliakoff creates a sense of what was loved and what has been lost.

I want to draw attention to one moment in this tale that is comprised of four shots. The first is a portrait shot of Alice as she narrates the tale to Daniel (see Figure 2.2). Alice is more austere in appearance than we have seen her before; wearing a plain grey shirt she is front lit from the kitchen window, the light appears natural but cold, picking out Alice's pale skin and gold hair from the gloomy kitchen behind her. Two long shelves of the kitchen dresser lined with blue and white willow pattern crockery run behind her in the frame. Through the sequence, Alice's narration and her image as its storyteller anchor the tale to the present both spatially and temporally, supported by the camera positioning and the logic of the shot construction. The camera is angled slightly to the left, a position constructed as part of the shot/reverse shot sequence with her listener, Daniel. This 'anchoring' is briefly disrupted by the next series of shots which articulate the irruption of memory.

Alice explains to Daniel that the numerous doctors seen by Richard all provided different and inconclusive diagnoses because 'he could be so charming when he wanted'. On making this statement in the shot just described, three quick taps on the window can be heard, interrupting the flow of the narration as a memory of the 'charming' Richard is called into being. It is possible that the tapping noise which startles Alice's memory is stimulated via the similar noise made by the builders in the upstairs apartment, referring to those sense impressions that stimulate memory and transport one back to the past. From focusing on Daniel, Alice's eyes flicker to the right to investigate the noise. Poliakoff cuts to the image of Richard rapping on the kitchen window pane. His sallow skin and the soft brown rings that encircle his blue eyes confirm his illness, but the framing and warm lighting of the young man invest his image with the charisma that Alice saw in him, and the sense of spontaneity and energy of his character is articulated by his sudden appearance at the window (see Figure 2.3). The collar of his iconic leather coat is pulled up around his neck, and he smiles in through the window. Poliakoff cuts back to a shot of Alice as she looks up to see who is tapping. We have moved into the past and are presented with a former version of Alice (see Figure 2.4); again she is seated at the kitchen table and the same crockery lines the shelves of the dresser, emphasising the sense of spatial continuity. However, a temporal shift is announced primarily through the change in costume and hairstyle; she is wearing lighter clothes, a soft beige V-necked jumper and her hair is longer and softer, tucked back behind her ears. These aspects of the changed mise-en-scène can certainly be read symbolically in terms of characterisation, where Alice is presented literally in two different lights depicting the character after and before her bereavement; firstly, in the gloomy austere light of a rainy afternoon and secondly, in the warm nostalgic glow of memory. This second version of Alice corresponds with the memory of Richard, emphasised again by a shift in camera angle from the left to the right and the logic of the point-of-view shot as Poliakoff cuts back again to the image of Richard smiling at the window.

Figure 2.3   Richard, past (*Perfect Strangers*, dir. Stephen Poliakoff, prod. Talkback for BBC, 2001).

Figure 2.4   Alice, past (*Perfect Strangers*, dir. Stephen Poliakoff, prod. Talkback for BBC, 2001).

Richard's present absence from the main narrative heightens the sense of haunting. The image of Richard in his long leather coat is littered through the drama, lending his appearance a certain iconic status. He exists in the space around Rebecca and Charles that Daniel senses but cannot quite fill himself and in his visible exclusion from the family tree. Daniel is unknowingly dressed up as Richard by Rebecca and Charles during the first evening of the reunion and significantly admits that the coat 'doesn't quite fit'. Even in the memory sequences, Richard's ghostly appearance, the sallow skin and ringed eyes, his leather cloak and unsettled demeanour, further compound his position as family spectre, and the repetition of his image in the final montage of memories exemplifies Alice's own private haunting.

Concluding her speech at the final dinner, Alice proposes that they drink 'to those who are no longer with us... those who couldn't be here'. It is at this point that Poliakoff reinserts the image of Richard smiling at the kitchen window. Its appearance is brief but extremely powerful, producing a sense of disorientation which visibly shakes Alice. Though the performance is extremely subtle, Alice/Duncan teeters back slightly and looks down, lost in the memory, and then up again as if realigning her perspective after being briefly jolted back to a different time and space.

The repetition of the image of Richard is referred to visually by this sequence but is also written into the dialogue after Daniel has engineered the confrontation between Rebecca, Charles and Alice. Daniel approaches Charles to apologise and as they both stand staring out over the formal gardens of the estate, Charles articulates his own sense of grief and guilt and explains how he is continually haunted by the image of Richard.

> Charles: Everyday I see him...
> Daniel: Richard?
> Charles: Yes...it doesn't matter where I am...last year I walked into a little supermarket in Mexico, and saw his face, suddenly by the counter, it was incredible.

The sudden 'reappearance' of Richard is described as a disruptive and powerful experience that mirrors the tremor experienced by Alice during her speech. These two examples of the repetitive and irruptive quality of memory operate as a powerful expression of its affective capacity.

Memory montages: 'Previously on' sequences and reflective codas

Through its use of montage and the employment of different still and moving image styles associated with different technologies of memory (e.g. domestic photography, home video), *Perfect Strangers* operates as an example of one of the 'many contemporary films, documentaries and television series [that] reframe (actual or fictive) home movie footage [...] either as a technique to create the illusion of intimacy and personal authenticity, or as a meta-commentary on the intertwining of memory and media' (van Dijck 2008, p. 72). Whilst *Perfect Strangers* successfully creates both this illusion and provides a similar form of commentary, it also operates as an example of a 'memory text'. Annette Kuhn writes that the form of the 'memory text' is 'characteristically collagist, fragmentary, timeless' and can 'call up, in words, or with the directness and apparent purity of sounds and images, a sense of what remembering feels like' (2000, p. 189). Memory texts in this sense invite empathy and identification, drawing upon our familiarity with the experience of memory.

Poliakoff effectively developed his use of montage in *Shooting the Past* (BBC, 1999) as a way of experimenting with photographic storytelling and slowing down television in order to create a memorable television experience (see Holdsworth 2006). What might be described as 'memory montages' in *Perfect Strangers* operate as part of the complex web of secrets that make up the drama's narrative but are also employed to effectively conjure that sense of what remembering feels like. In this analysis I shall refer in detail to two 'memory montages' from the last episode of *Perfect Strangers*: the first opens the episode and the second appears in the final scene of the series.

In *Perfect Strangers*, Poliakoff extends his use of memory technologies, from the use of still photography in *Shooting the Past*, to incorporate sections of film which are intended to be home movie footage. These sections are signalled as such by the grainy texture of the film stock (the use of video and Super 8). These 'dated' styles of photography and film provide the viewer with a series of images that are repeated throughout the drama, often irrupting into characters' dreams and fantasies. In the opening of the third episode a montage of memories from the different family stories accompanies the credits. In a way it may be read as a 'previously on...' sequence, a practice familiar from serial drama, reminding the viewer of the stories discovered so far. The connections between the stories which are revealed at the end of the drama are inferred at this point by placing the 'memories' together along with an extract from the diagram of the Symon family tree. The relationships between the characters and their stories are also emphasised by the mirroring of shots. The camera pans up the film image of the young Daniel dressed in his 'little prince' outfit, from the decorated slippers to the wide-eyed face of the boy fidgeting with his ruffled collar. A similar camera movement pans up the still photographic image of the young Raymond and then up the figure of his father stood next to him, the similarities between the father and son evidenced in their identical posturing.

Characters are compelled to uncover the meaning behind certain images and photographs as memory and fantasy combine in order to reconstruct their histories. There is a simultaneous weaving and unravelling of story, image and meaning in *Perfect Strangers* which is threaded together by what Sarah Cardwell calls an 'intermedia, cross-temporal montage' (2005, p. 185), but what we might refer to here, however, as the 'texture of memory' as it corresponds with Kuhn's idea of the collagist and fragmentary nature of the memory text. The sequence pieces together the fragments of memory, represented here by different styles of film and photography, not only to create a sense of the texture of memory but also in order to piece together elements of the narrative puzzle.

If the above example operates as a 'previously on' sequence, the example below is reminiscent of the reflective codas that are employed across serial drama and other televisual forms. Here, the use of montage and music is key to the orchestration of the moment.[6] Having gathered at the old family estate, now a conference centre and golf course, for the final function of the reunion, and after Daniel's failed attempt to reconcile Alice and the siblings, and the revelation of Raymond's father's secret life, the family sits down together at a long banquet table. Sitting at the head of the table, Alice is invited to make a speech. After the usual formalities, Alice's words prompt a final memory montage, operating as a summary of the drama's key stories and characters.

> Alice: Some of you will remember this house, some of you may have been here as children...And also there are many of you here who attended the reunion and who have come face to face with memories...We will all have our own private list of course.

This memory sequence is once again characterised by the devices of irruption and repetition that, as I have argued, simulate the activity or rhythm of memory in the text and mark the continued elision between the past and present. From the cut from Alice to Raymond remembering, to the cut back from Rebecca's memory of a younger Alice, the montage sequence lasts 45 seconds and contains 22 shots. Similar to montage sequences in Poliakoff's earlier drama, *Shooting the Past*, the pace of the scene is constructed through editing not camera work. Its hypnotic effect is induced by the measured pace – each frame lasting approximately two seconds – and heightened by the evocative score featuring the repetitive refrain of the piano. The tide-like movement between past and present, with each frame of memory anchored to its character, supports the sense of privatisation, yet each character is sharing the experience of remembering. Alice's words themselves ('we will *all* have our own *private* list of course') point towards the quality of the sequence as an articulation of both private history/memory and collective experience, indicating the complexity of memory formation with regards to television as both private viewing experience and cultural form. At the close of Alice's speech, nothing is articulated, but a series of eye-line matches between Daniel and Alice, and Alice and the siblings signal both appreciation and the possibility of reconciliation. This is accompanied by the movement in the score, from the recurring and repetitive theme of the drama, characterised by Cardwell as sustaining a sense of 'holding off' (Cardwell 2005, p. 184), of crescendo without climax, to a gentler and drifting piano accompaniment. As with *Shooting the Past*, the drama achieves a sense of closure without completion, and one might also argue that space is made for the viewer at the Symon family reunion. As the family toasts to Alice's speech, the camera is located at the opposite end of the long banquet table. This position is taken up again in the last shot of the drama. As Irving stands on a table to take a photograph of the gathered family members, they all turn to face the camera and the viewer. Whilst this shot might be signalled as Irving's point of view behind the camera, the direct-to-camera address calls the viewer into being, situating them as part of the family, whilst leaving open a space for the viewer to bring with them their own family ghosts and memories.

What I wanted to consider in relation to the analysis of *Perfect Strangers* as a memory text is how the depiction of acts of memory and remembrance within the drama, the presentation of a texture and activity of memory, based on the assumption that they are relatable experiences, might evoke our own acts and practices of memory and memorialisation. This argument is based on the understanding that television operates as part of a system of *everyday* memory-making, drawn from its role in daily life and the dynamics of the home. The space of the home is also often filled with the fragments of memory. For example, just as photographs littered the space of the archive in *Shooting the Past*, the mise-en-scène of *Perfect Strangers* is saturated with family photographs which line the furniture in the characters' homes. Television often sits within this everyday memory network and this could indeed have consequences for the viewing experience of, in this instance, family dramas about personal history and memory viewed within a family space covered with history and memory. The ghosts invoked by the stories told might very well be our own.

Whilst *Perfect Strangers* might be described as an example of 'art television',[7] there are many features and moments within the three-part drama that are reminiscent of or rework the characteristics of long-running serial drama. As I move on to consider how moments of return and retreat, of repetition and repetition with a difference work in relation to longer forms of serial drama, I am not unaware of the hierarchies of value that exist in relation to the objects of study I have selected – art 'v' popular, melodrama 'v' realism. There are certainly formal commonalities across all the examples which I attempt to emphasise, but perhaps most importantly I want to write about these examples *as television* – to consider the (medium) specific ways in which memory is employed and evoked.

ER (NBC, 1994–2009)

Set in the emergency room of the fictional County General Hospital in Chicago, *ER* broke the mould of the hospital drama when it launched in 1994. It delivered huge ratings and received much critical acclaim though the show noticeably tired and eventually ran its course, bowing out at the end of its fifteenth season as the longest running medical series on prime-time television in the US. There were numerous 'moments' in the final season as the show became increasingly self-conscious of its own memory. For example, a secret 'memorial wall', in the basement of the hospital, was discovered by the characters Abby (Maura Tierney) and Neela (Parminder Nagra) at the beginning and end of the season respectively, bookmarking and emphasising the finality of the programme.[8] The final episode itself self-consciously mirrored the structure of the 'pilot', charting 24 hours in the life of the emergency room. As an ending there was an insistence on the 'everyday' time of the hospital as cyclical and repetitive, where life ends and begins. This is particularly apparent in not only the births and deaths within the emergency room, but also the explicit marking of the serial drama's system of generational replacement. Dr John Carter's (Noah Wyle) first day at County General, in the pilot, is mirrored by *Gilmore Girl* Alexis Bledel introduced as the new intern Dr Julia Wise, struggling through her own first day. The presence/absence of deceased Dr Greene resonates through repeated imagery – the opening shot of the pilot which introduced Greene is reproduced; only now it is Archie Morris (Scott Grimes) who occupies the quiet and darkened treatment room.[9] Greene's daughter Rachel (Hallee Hirsch), now 22, also arrives as a prospective medical student. There were a series of returning characters and guest appearances in the finale and in other episodes across the final season. The episode 'Old Times' saw the much-anticipated return of Dr Doug Ross (George Clooney) and nurse Carol Hathaway (Julianna Margulies).[10] Even deceased characters such as Dr Mark Greene (Anthony Edwards) and Dr Robert Romano (Paul McCrane) reappeared through a series of flashback sequences attached to the storyline of a new doctor Cate Banfield (Angela Bassett), who recalled her previous experience of the emergency room as a mother whose son was brought in and subsequently died. It is this episode that I want to look at in more detail.

The original transmission of 'Heal Thyself' (season 15, episode 7, tx: 14 November 2008) was itself framed as a memorial space. Broadcast the week after the death of series creator Michael Crichton, the episode opens with a short eulogy read by original cast member Eriq La Salle (Dr Peter Benton).[11] The creation of a reflective mood, though unintentional, complements the themes of the episode and its development of character – opening as it does on an overhead close-up of Cate Banfield, lying on her bed and lost in thought as her husband is heard calling out to her. Banfield is brought in as the new 'chief of the ER' in episode two of season 15. As a character she is initially depicted as cold, serious and secretive, immediately ruffling the feathers of more established staff members of the emergency room. 'Heal Thyself' is structured through a series of flashbacks which are clearly presented as Cate's memory. The episode reveals a key event in the character's history and acts as an explanation for Cate's dour and frosty demeanour – a demeanour which is re-read in the light of memory as troubled by guilt and grief. In the episode, Cate's 'present-day' treatment of a near-drowned little girl and her handling of the girl's mother and grandfather is paralleled with her previous experience of the emergency room, where her son is treated by Dr Greene. In the flashback scenes we see Cate struggling with the slippage between her own professional and personal roles as both doctor and mother, and with the self-blame of not having spotted her son's condition sooner. In the present-day scenes we see Cate draw upon this experience, and in particular the example set by Greene, to influence her own treatment of the little girl and her family.

The shift between present day and flashback narratives are signalled via a variety of devices. Fragments of dialogue and image matches (the throwing of a football, a close-up of the mother's hand gripping the child's), shifts in mood and tone (the urgency of the trauma room, the mothers' fear, the grandfather's guilt) – all work to summon and suture the elisions between past and present. Each flashback is also specifically anchored to Cate as the episode presents us with her experience of 'remembering', but 'Heal Thyself' also summons and invokes an additional form of remembering in the reappearance of Mark Greene. The much-loved and respected former 'chief of the ER' died of a brain tumour in a protracted and painful storyline in season eight of the series. It is on the moment of Greene's return that I want to focus here.

As the girl's treatment progresses in the present and as the son's condition becomes more serious in the past, the flashbacks begin to appear more frequently. Midway through the episode Cate and her son speed to the hospital in an ambulance. Framed in a medium close-up shot, Cate anxiously watches her son and clutches his hand. After the off-screen paramedic announces their arrival at County General, we hear the ambulance doors opening, and as Cate looks up the white sun lights up the frame accompanied by a subtle shift in musical tone from minor to major. There is a cut here to Cate's point of view. Looking down at Cate, his arms outstretched as he pulls back the doors, a flare of sunlight from left of frame gives the familiar figure of Mark Greene an ethereal glow as he announces – 'Welcome to County General. I'm Doctor Greene.' There is a sense in which the shift in musical tone and lighting of the scene at this moment anticipate Greene's return and there is certainly a self-consciousness to the presentation of the returning tragic hero, with lighting and positioning giving the character a messianic quality (see Figure 2.5).[12]

As the episode progresses it becomes clear how Cate's memory instructs her own action in the present day. In one significant shot, whilst breaking the 'realism' of the show, Greene's role within the episode as both ghost and guide, existing in both past and present, is evoked. Following Greene's reappearance and back in the present day Cate performs a thoracotomy on the young girl. As her mother cries, 'why isn't anything working?' there is a cut to a close-up of Cate. As she looks to her left the camera moves with her glance, and behind her in long shot, bathed in a pool of light in the darkened recesses of the room, Dr Greene stands, putting on surgical gloves. Speaking *to* Cate in the past and *for* Cate in the present, he remarks – 'we're just getting started here' – and the flashback narrative resumes.

It is here that the episode begins to cross-cut more rapidly between past and present as the two trauma cases, though in different temporal zones, run parallel in adjoining hospital treatment rooms. Whilst the cross-cutting between patients/storylines is a common structural device within serial drama (see Newman 2006), here it is also cross-temporal

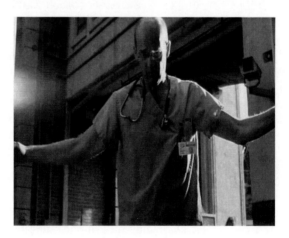

Figure 2.5   Mark Greene, 'Heal Thyself', *ER*, season 15, episode 7 (dir. David Zabel, prod. Constant c Productions/Amblin Television/Warner Bros.Television, US, 2008).

as the past and present are rhymed and aligned via movement (a nurse walks from one room to the next), action (medical kits are ripped open) and dialogue (the listing of medications). Whilst the move between past and present is facilitated by action and sound (the beeping of machines and a quiet emotive score underlining the scene), the past and the present are also distinguished as separate events, principally through Cate's different hairstyles (long with a fringe in the past, and a short crop in the present) and the different coloured tiles of the two trauma rooms (yellow in the past and green in the present).

Cate's interactions and treatment in the present are paralleled *and* informed by her memory of her own interactions with Dr Greene. For example, Greene asks if it is possible her son ingested something and the memory of this question sparks Cate to reconsider the little girl's case as she questions her team – 'Maybe it's an ingestion?' Whilst Cate's son dies and the girl lives, Cate's memory is an instructive one and she affirms her earlier rationalisation to a despondent junior doctor – 'There's no way to be ready for something like this, but in the end it'll make you better – you can't be a great doctor until you've killed a patient.'

There are a number of associative possibilities generated across this episode for characterisation and storytelling. The memory structure works to insert the new character of Cate with the resonance of a longer series history, and there is a layering of pathos within her momentary encounter with the dying Greene. Various moments in the episode summon a series memory of his condition: Greene winces and puts his hand to his head, and a series of reaction shots become loaded with the accumulated knowledge of his character's history and future. But here new meanings are also generated within old contexts, and new characters, such as Cate Banfield, are lent the weight of history and memory.

Both this particular episode and the other 'memorial devices' within the final season – the encounters between past and present characters and performers, the repetition of storylines and character types (the 'chief', the new intern, etc.) – can be seen to provoke a series of comparative gestures. In terms of television memory and nostalgia, they offer a commentary on 'who we were and how we have changed' but they also illuminate the potential comparative function of serial storytelling. Where we see roles filled by new actors and storylines repurposed, features of seriality and repetition allow the viewer and critic to evaluate aspects of performance, storytelling and characterisation across the life of a series.

Grey's Anatomy (ABC, 2005–)

Writing of the device of 'thematic parallelism' in the prime-time serial, Newman comments that 'it would seem an obvious one when dealing with multiple storylines: have them inflect and play off each other, revealing contrasts and similarities' (2006, p. 21). Whilst 'thematic parallelism' is a widespread storytelling device, Jason Jacobs' work on hospital drama reveals its specific function within this particular genre. He employs the term 'reflectors' for patients who 'operate as dramatic "reflectors" for the medical staff by representing or articulating dimensions of their predicament, identity or situation that is reflected back to them in an acute form' (2003, p. 14). For Jacobs, ' "reflectors" implies the sense of return as to reflect means to cast back – where the main characters are often provoked into introspection or a change of mind by the actions, thoughts and feelings of their patients' (2003, pp. 119–20).[13]

Another ensemble hospital drama but in a very different mode, *Grey's Anatomy*, currently in its seventh season, is set within the surgery unit at the fictional Seattle Grace Hospital. Described by one of its characters as 'High School with scalpels',[14] it is as indebted to teen drama as it is the hospital drama and the interpersonal and romantic relationships between the doctors are very much at the centre of the melodrama. Whilst patients operate in the same way as the 'reflectors' of *ER*, the doctors at Seattle Grace Hospital are often framed in doorways, watching, listening, witnessing, on the periphery of their patients' lives. The drama of patients' lives unfolding is often intercut with reaction shots of the doctors to signpost their empathetic response and to signal moments of reflection and identification for the central characters. But where *Grey's Anatomy* might seem to differ is in the multiple layering of these reflective relationships, where characters are continually prompted to reflect upon their own tangled romances and friendships. This sets up a distinctive set of patterns and rhymes within the show that point towards a manipulative, melodramatic and playful use of repetition and series memory.

The idea of the 'moment' within *Grey's Anatomy* is as self-conscious as its construction in the memorial moments in the concluding season of *ER*. But here the term also takes on a promotional function; a mid season three clip show is called 'Every Moment Counts' and the DVD release of the fifth season promises to offer the viewer 'more moments'. As I discuss elsewhere the idea of the 'memorable moment' is central to forms of nostalgia programming, and processes of memorialisation occur through DVD features and the repetitive forms of the clip show. It is the repetitive forms of the patterns and rhymes that feature across the text of *Grey's Anatomy* that I want to move on to consider.

The construction of dialogue in *Grey's Anatomy* is central to the tone and character of the show. Significantly, and revealing the strong female address of the show, the series is framed by the voice-over of its central character, Dr Meredith Grey (Ellen Pompeo). The voice-overs themselves operate within a reflective mode, deliberating on the trials of life, death and love; a mode which is further emphasised by the common use of speeches. These are highly charged moments which foreground performance but are lent a dramatic intensity through the repetitive use of language and the construction of a poetic rhythm.[15] Designed not to mimic the natural patterns of speech – they are not disruptive, breaking the narrative flow – but they are points of emotional emphasis and revelation which often propel the narrative and character arc forward and whilst they work to foreground an emotional point, they also resonate and draw parallels between these various arcs. At the centre of the ensemble of characters and storylines is the on/off romance between Meredith and Dr Derek Shepherd (Patrick Dempsey). When Derek's estranged wife unexpectedly arrives at Seattle Grace Hospital, at the end of season one, Meredith throws her hat into the ring and asks Derek to – 'Pick me. Choose me. Love me'.[16] Whilst this 'moment' of vulnerability reverberates across her character arc (Derek doesn't choose her, initially) we see her words returned to in Derek's speech from the opening of season three, where he admits he chose wrong. In Meredith's kitchen the characters face one another for the first time since they had sex at the hospital prom at the end of season two (the night before in terms of the plot),[17] and Meredith repeats the question asked by Derek in the previous episode – 'So what does this mean?'

> Derek: It means you have a choice. You have a *choice to make*, and I don't want to rush you into making a decision before you're ready. This morning I was *gonna come over*, I was *gonna say*, what I wanted to *say* was... but now all I can *say* is that... I'm in *love with you*. I've been in *love with you* for, I don't know... I'm a *little late*, I know I'm a *little late* to tell you that. I just, I just want you to *take your time*, y'know, *take all the time* you need because you have a *choice to make* and when I had a *choice to make* I chose wrong.
>
> (My emphasis, 'Time Has Come Today', season 3, episode 1)

The pattern of the speech develops a distinct beat through the successive repetitions of key words and phrases ('love with you', 'little late', 'take your time'). It is both circular, returning to the line 'choice to make', and open-ended, leaving Meredith to make the decision which develops the storyline. Derek's declaration also resonates across the storyline of Dr Isobel 'Izzie' Stevens (Katherine Heigl) and the heart patient with whom she falls in love, Denny Duquette (Jeffrey Dean Morgan). In the season two finale, after Izzie has risked her career and Denny's life to secure his place at the top of the heart transplant list, Denny makes a similar declaration to the young doctor.

> Denny: For five years I've had to live by the *choices* of my doctors. The guys that cut me open decided my life. There wasn't one *choice* that was mine. And now I have this heart that beats and works. I get to be like everybody else. I get to make my own decisions, have my own life. Do whatever the damn hell I *choose*. Now here's the good part, so you listen close. What I *choose* is you. You're who I want to wake up with and go to bed with and do everything inbetween with. I get a *choice* now. I get to *choose*. I *choose* you, Izzie Stevens.
>
> (My emphasis, 'Losing my Religion', season 2, episode 27)

The context and the style of each speech are similar. The finale and the premiere were both written by show creator Shonda Rhimes, and they are certainly not the only occasions when a repetitive use of language is employed. Work on soap opera reminds us how repetition and recapitulation operate as a way to remind viewers of narrative events. Here these techniques work in similar and additional ways: they operate as a bridge between the ending of season two and opening of season three but they are also part of the dense and self-conscious layering of resonances and associations. As 'moments' of declaration they feel neat and self-contained, melodramatically charged through the use of reaction shots and the slow move to close-up. They often close on a reaction shot of the addressee and prompt that character's need for further reflection.

Beginnings and endings, premieres and finales are interesting spaces within the life of a serial drama. The bridging of old and new storylines, where endings are often beginnings, is arguably a key characteristic of opening and closing episodes. Similar to the *ER* finale and across *Grey's Anatomy*, there is an insistence on cyclicality as a pattern of folding and unfolding emerges. Seasons three and five in particular are bookended by mirroring scenes which draw parallels, shape and interweave specific narrative and character arcs. In season five, a patient's experience of short-term memory loss in the two-part premiere is repeated in the finale, only this time it is as Izzie, having been diagnosed with advanced melanoma which has spread to her brain, awakens from surgery with the same condition.

Season three opens with the aftermath of the hospital prom and Izzie is catatonic on the floor of the bathroom following Denny's sudden death at the end of season two.[18] She remains in her prom dress (distinctly reminiscent of a bridal gown) in this position for the duration of the episode. It is not until the final musical coda that she pulls herself off the floor and Meredith helps her out of her dress. This is mirrored by a scene in the final episode of season three in which fiercely independent Dr Cristina Yang (Sandra Oh), jilted at the altar by her partner and fellow surgeon Dr Preston Burke (Isaiah Washington), returns with Meredith to their apartment to find his treasured possessions gone.[19] Realising he has gone for good, she stands in the middle of the room and exhales – 'He's gone. I'm free. Damn it, damn it.'

She breaks down, the music swells on the soundtrack and she struggles to rip off her corseted dress and choker. It is here that Meredith, once again, helps her friend to shed the garment, this time with increased urgency and the aid of a pair of scissors. The dress in both examples has a clear symbolic significance and given that we see the characters in scrubs for the majority of the time, the spectacle of witnessing the characters 'dressed up' is arguably as significant as the narrative context of the shift in costume. These moments do not, however, rest upon the conventional pleasures of the transformation sequence, as the prom and the wedding dress become associated with bereavement and loss.

Though writing in the context of serial killer films, Richard Dyer comments that 'seriality emphasises anticipation, suspense, what will happen next? It also emphasises repetition, pattern, structure' (2000 (1997), p. 146). Pattern and the anticipation of repetition become part of the pleasures of seriality within *Grey's Anatomy*. Repetition functions not just to generate resonances and allusive meaning – those invokings that prompt a 'fresh charge of feeling' for experienced viewers (Newman 2006, p. 19) – but they work to build anticipation and suspense; what will happen next? How will the pattern fit together?

I return here to the night of the hospital prom, the moment of Denny's death and the appearance of Izzie in her prom dress. Alone in his room and awaiting the arrival of Izzie, his new fiancée, Denny suffers a fatal stroke. A close-up on the flatline of his heart monitor dissolves into a camera pan from left to right as the line of the monitor merges with the tiles on the wall outside the hospital elevator. Continuing to pan right the moving frame reveals Izzie in the elevator, wrapped in a deep pink dress with bandeau top and full, floor-skimming skirt, her

Figure 2.6   Izzie Stevens, 'Losing my Religion', *Grey's Anatomy*, season 2, episode 27 (dir. Mark Tinker, prod. Mark Gordon Productions/ShondaLand/Touchstone Television, US, 2006).

blonde hair gathered up in loose chignon and small diamante droplets in her ears. She leans forward to press the elevator button then gathers up the trail of her dress, and with nervous anticipation she runs the fabric through her hands as the door closes and the scene fades to black (see Figure 2.6). Sutured by a graphic match, the continuing tone of the flatline and the soft indie ballad on the soundtrack ('Grace' by Kate Havnevik), Denny's death and Izzie's anticipation are cruelly juxtaposed with the preceding sex scene between Meredith and Derek and the sense of dramatic irony heightened by the use of the lyric 'I just want to feel your embrace' over Izzie's anticipation in the elevator.

In the musical coda at the end of 'Dream a Little Dream of Me, pt 2', the second episode of season five, Izzie steps out onto the corridor outside her bedroom to see Alex Karev (Justin Chambers), her colleague, roommate and on/off lover, flaunting his latest conquest. Accompanied by a soft indie ballad that weaves together the multiple storylines across the coda, the medium close-up of Izzie bleaches out and returns to the scene on the night of the prom as she enters the elevator holding the trail of her gown. As the camera tracks in she pushes the button and the doors close. We cut to a close-up of Izzie inside the elevator. Here, her expression is one of a relaxed excitement without the anxiety that marked the earlier version of the scene (see Figure 2.7). As the doors open, a point-of-view shot reveals a smiling Denny waiting for her. As Izzie beams back she tells him – 'See I told you I would show you my dress', to which he responds – 'you look better than the bride'. Hand in hand they walk down the corridor and into the light. Bleaching out

Figure 2.7 Izzie Stevens, 'Dream a Little Dream of Me, pt 2', *Grey's Anatomy*, season 5, episode 2 (dir. Ron Corn, prod. ShondaLand/The Mark Gordon Company/ABC Studios, US, 2008).

the frame the scene dissolves back to Izzie outside her bedroom and as Alex closes the door behind him, Meredith's voice-over announces that 'fairytales don't come true. Reality is much stormier.'

Whilst clearly referencing back and relying on the resonance of the earlier version of the scene and its significance for the character, its reappearance also has a prophetic quality and points towards the new season's storylines; Denny does, in fact, return. In a device designed to unsettle the audience and signal Izzie's illness, Denny returns to Izzie as a ghost/hallucination and competes with Alex for her affection.[20] The explanation for the scenario, which could be read as an excuse to capitalise on the popularity of the characters and the desire to see their relationship consummated, is left open and leads towards the revelation that Izzie has 'terminal' cancer; Denny either returns to warn Izzie of her illness or is a manifestation of that illness.

It is within the context of this particular story arc that the elevator scene is returned to for a third time in the musical coda at the close of the season five finale which binds together two specific storylines. First, Izzie, now married to Alex, awakens from brain surgery with short-term memory loss. Despite the initial anxiety which recalls a patient from the opening of the season, she appears to begin to recover. Secondly, a 'John Doe' in a critical condition and with severe facial injuries is brought into the hospital. He is revealed towards the end of the episode to be series regular George O'Malley (TR Knight), Izzie's best friend and former lover who was leaving Seattle Grace Hospital to join the army. In the final moments of the episode both characters become asystolic.[21]

The transmission of the season five finale was inevitably informed by the publicity that one or both of the actors would be leaving the series, effectively heightening the anticipation and tension as the episode concludes with both characters' lives hanging in the balance. The coda cuts between the attempts to save Izzie and George and as the soundtrack builds in intensity and volume, the speed of the cuts between the two resuscitation teams is also intensified; sutured by both the music, the electric tone of the flat-lining heart monitor and Meredith's voice-over – 'Did you say it? I love you. I don't ever wanna live without you. You changed my life. Did you say it? Make a plan, set a goal, work toward it. But every now and then look around, drink it in...'

An overhead, close-up of an unconscious Izzie bleaches out to white and the dissolve returns us, once again, to the character in her iconic deep pink gown as she enters the elevator. With a more washed out colour palette, the tone of the image is slightly different to the earlier versions of the scene, in particular the sunny second version of the scene as a fantasy reunion with Denny.

In this version, Izzie's expression is anxious and troubled as the elevator becomes symbolic of a space in between life and death (see Figure 2.8). Following the same pattern of shots as the second version, the cut from Izzie to her point of view anticipates a final reunion with Denny and the fulfilment of his prophecy – 'I'm here *for* you Izzie Stevens.'[22] The emotional crescendo of the scene is revealed as the soundtrack breaks for the chorus; the doors open and there stands George, regenerated and transformed, pristine in his army uniform

Figure 2.8   Izzie Stevens, 'Now or Never', *Grey's Anatomy*, season 5, episode 24 (dir. Ron Corn, prod. ShondaLand/The Mark Gordon Company/ABC Studios, US, 2009).

complete with buzz cut. There is no exchange of dialogue as editing, music (the specially written 'Off I Go' by Greg Laswell) and performance build the season cliffhanger. The shot-reverse shot between Izzie and George is intercut with shots of them under resuscitation. The scene is clearly framed as Izzie's subconscious. As George warmly smiles at Izzie and she tentatively smiles back, the noise of the defibrillator breaks her concentration and she glances away. The choice between life and death is clearly marked as hers and the coda concludes with a return to the overhead close-up of Izzie as her head jolts back as electricity fires through her body. The final cut to black is concluded by Meredith's closing voice-over – '... because, this is it. It might all be gone tomorrow.'

I have chosen to write about these scenes at length because they reveal to me a different way of understanding the operation of memory, different to the repetition of key moments in the memory montage or the representations of remembering. Here, the elaborate and self-conscious layering of associations and resonances is captured by the patterned return to and reversioning of a brief scene. The scene is reconstructed and revised twice, wrong-footing the audience's expectations each time. The density of these repetitions and revisions also makes the attempt to explain the narrative context of each moment a difficult project. Again the weight of character history is summoned by the sequence – the death-defying relationship between Izzie and Denny, the close relationship between Izzie and George – a relationship that intensifies across season three by their shared experience of bereavement; Izzie loses Denny and George loses his father. The resonance of the dress and the dramatic use of costume are also central, becoming emotional markers and identifying the scenes as moments of heightened melodrama.

To return to Julian Wolfreys, writing on Victorian literature and informed by Derrida's work on the spectral, he argues that:

> what returns is never simply a repetition that recalls an anterior origin or presence, but is always an iterable supplement: repetition with a difference. There is, then, an apparently circular or, more precisely, a folding and unfolding motion which in the act of appearing to complete itself moves us somewhere else, so that what we come to read on so many occasions is a figure, to borrow Tennyson's words, *of the same, but not the same.*
>
> (2002, p. 19)

Whilst none of the dramas I discuss adopt this mode, there is the potential here for an uncanny rendering of the moment of return, where the familiar becomes strange, of the same but not the same. Repetition with a difference, though, is central to the function of these scenes. Whilst looping back and emphasising the significance of the moment, they push the narrative forward as the narrative pattern plays with the (emotional) expectations it has established.

The Wire (HBO, 2002–8)

Continuing the discussion of the significance of endings and beginnings within these contemporary serial dramas, I want to conclude this chapter with a final example from the home of American 'quality programming', HBO.[23] The much-celebrated drama *The Wire* has been considered to be the closest thing on television to literature, applauded by critics and referred to by its creators as a 'visual novel' (see Mittell 2008, p. 429). Here, commentary returns the serial storytelling of the drama back to its roots in nineteenth-century culture and the serialised novels of Dickens et al. It is not a narrative I wish to trace here. What interests me is how the features of seriality and their relationship to time and memory – the repetitions and cycles, the sense of endlessness – also become thematic concerns within the five-season drama.

Throughout the series we witness the inability of characters to break or escape the behavioural and environmental cycles that they are imprisoned in. This becomes most apparent in the pattern of generational replacement set up within the show, as the boys introduced in season four become different chess pieces within the game – junkie, soldier, cop, stick-up man. The players change but the game remains the same. This, according to Marsha Kinder (2008) affords some kind of hope. Long-term addict Bubbles (Andre Royo) eventually joins his sister at the family table; one of the boys, Namond (Julito McCullum), is fostered by ex-District Commander Bunny Colvin (Robert Wisdom) (though this might be more a case of switching sides rather than escaping the game). However, the disposability of the players and the replacement and repetition of roles are evoked in a reflective speech from the treacherous henchman Cheese (Method Man) in the series finale:

> See that? See now that's just the wrong way to look at it, coz Joe had his time and Omar put an end to that. Then Marlo had his time, short as it was, and the police put an end to that. And now motherfucker, it's our time. Mines and yours. But instead of kicking in, you gonna stand there cryin' that back in the day shit. There ain't no back in the

day, nigger. Ain't no nostalgia to this shit here. There's just the street
and the game and what happen here today.

('-30-', season 5, episode 10)

In full rhetorical flow Cheese is shot in the head at point-blank range as
payback for his betrayal of Proposition Joe (Robert F. Chew).[24] Having
worked his way up the ranks he is killed and discarded, and as the collective drive away, another corpse is left littering another patch of West
Baltimore wasteland.

Here the device of 'generational replacement', common across long-
running series and evident in *ER* and *Grey's Anatomy*, carries a political
and sociological dimension as part of a portrait of a city and a study
of environmental determinism. Other serial storytelling devices are also
apparent: the reflective relationship between police and drug dealers,
the recurrence of key words and phrases that run across the show like a
musical refrain (see Kinder 2008, p. 57). For example, Detective Jimmy
McNulty's (Dominic West) exclamation 'what the fuck did I do?' is
repeated across the first series and the resonance of West's performance
of the line shifts from an arrogant absence of responsibility in the opening episode, to a deep sense of guilt following the near-fatal shooting of
his colleague Kima (Sonja Sohn) in the penultimate instalment.

Whilst it was praised for its realism, *The Wire* presented a concluding montage at the end of each season which, whilst working to offer
some sense of closure to the individual series and its specific storylines,
pointed towards new and continuing narrative threads and was suggestive of the ways in which 'life goes on'.[25] They were also moments
which foregrounded the 'construction' of the programme and illustrated
Jason Mittell's observations on the narrative complexity and spectacle
of contemporary television drama in which he suggests 'we watch these
shows not just to get swept away in a realistic narrative world [...] but
also to watch the gears at work, marvelling at the craft required to pull
off such narrative pyrotechnics' (2006, p. 35). The self-consciousness of
these sequences is signalled here by the rare use of a non-diegetic soundtrack – the choice of music temporally framing the montage not entirely
dissimilar to the use of the musical coda at the end of a show such as
Grey's Anatomy.

The season two and season five finales were interesting in that the
montage sequence was anchored to a specific character.[26] Constructed
via the logic of the flashback, whilst creating the sense that 'life goes
on', the function of these sequences is to insist upon the sense of the

imprisonment and powerlessness of the individual against the corruption and criminality of American society and government – visually enacting the themes of movement and stasis. It is the heavily symbolic image of Nick Sobotka (Pablo Schreiber), nephew of the corrupted and subsequently murdered Stevedore Union leader Frank Sobotka (Chris Bauer), clinging to and framed behind a wire fence which anchors season two's concluding montage (see Figure 2.9).

The image intentionally mirrors an image of Frank in the previous episode, recalling Nick's final encounter with his uncle (see Figure 2.10).[27] Season two's focus on the Port of Baltimore, the decline of industry and its effect on a male, white, working-class community is entwined with notions of decay and loss, and this sequence, accompanied by the country–rock track 'I Feel Alright' by Steve Earle, concludes with an accelerating montage of images of the empty and derelict dockyards, before returning to the image of Nick. His uncle murdered and his cousin in jail, Nick fails to escape the port through illegitimate or legitimate means and the symbolic effect of Nick's entrapment behind the fence, overlooking the closed factories, is exaggerated by a return to diegetic sound – the silence of the port and the quiet rain falling.

Discussing the image of Mark Greene in the first season of *ER*, Jacobs argues 'that final image is haunted by the possibilities of his future' (2001, p. 437). Similarly, here, the final image of Nick is haunted by both the past and a lost future. And this is not the last time we see Nick – the

Figure 2.9 Nick Sobotka, 'Port in a Storm', *The Wire*, season 2, episode 12 (dir. Robert F. Colesberry, prod. Blown Deadline Productions/HBO, US, 2003).

Figure 2.10 Frank Sobotka, 'Bad Dreams', *The Wire*, season 2, episode 11 (dir. Ernest R. Dickerson, prod. Blown Deadline Productions/HBO, US, 2003).

character very briefly reappears in season five, heckling Mayor Carcetti (Aidan Gillen) at the opening of a new port regeneration project.[28] In this appearance he is now a relic, a leftover from season two, but he brings with him a set of character and narrative associations and resonances. With an irony that belies the significance of this appearance for the viewer, but equally a commentary on the character's declining status in the 'real world', Nick is escorted away by security as the Mayor turns to his aide – 'Who the hell's that?' – 'it's nobody Mr Mayor. Nobody at all.'

We might consider the ways in which these fragments, the reappearance of Nick, or the tattered campaign poster image of tragic union leader Frank, become affective triggers. The latter is an image that is purposefully, yet fleetingly focused upon in a short one-shot scene in the concluding montage of season three. The camera pans over a billboard stapled with the tattered re-election posters and then opens out to reveal Omar (Michael K. Williams) throwing the gun that killed Stringer Bell (Idris Elba) into the dockland waters. Layers of associations and meanings can be generated in the meeting of storylines within this moment, and the poster acts as a memory-trace weighted with meaning for the committed viewer.

The moment of return can be commemorative, melodramatic or poignantly fleeting, as in these examples from *The Wire*, or in the passing image of Nate's reflection in *Six Feet Under*. Self-consciously brief and underplayed they evoke, once again, Julian Wolfreys' thoughts on the ghostly movement of narrative; a folding and unfolding action which is perhaps best characterised by the brevity of these momentary appearances, the layering of traces, and the return and retreat that enacts a rhythm of ebb and flow, which, to me, seems so central to television, its pleasures and rewards. It is also, for me, a rhythm which still exists even with the emergence of new forms of consumption, such as the DVD box set. Whilst we have more control over the pattern of return, texts still repeatedly come into and out of our lives. It is a phenomenon that has made the forms, functions and pleasures of repetition even more fascinating and which I shall continue to investigate in Chapters 4 and 5 of this book. Whilst I have attempted to link the examples in this chapter through the analysis of representations of reflection and remembering, systems of generational replacement and the generation of patterns and resonances, they are also all examples which offer us representations of loss. For me, these moments of return have the potential to 'link us to our losses', both within the text but also beyond it, to our lives lived as a backdrop to the stories television tells.

3
Who Do You Think You Are? Memory and Identity in the Family History Documentary

The popularity of family history research as a national pastime has been successfully adopted by British television over the last five years, with *Who Do You Think You Are?* (*WDYTYA*), produced by Wall to Wall, pioneering the employment of family history and memory as a televisual narrative strategy. The first series aired in autumn 2004 to popular and critical acclaim, becoming one of the highest-rated shows on BBC Two. It was promoted to BBC One in 2006 and is currently, at the time of writing, in its seventh series, bringing the total number of episodes to 60. The success of the format, which follows the genealogical investigations of various television personalities as they track down the stories behind their family trees, may indeed have convinced commissioners that, according to *WDYTYA* alumnus Ian Hislop, 'family history is not dull, but a surprisingly watchable commodity' (in Rowan 2005, p. 12). As Vanessa Thorpe commented in *The Observer*, 'the British now love family history research as much as they love gardening or DIY' (Thorpe 2004). Certainly not only a British phenomenon though, the format has found international success, selling to broadcasters across Western Europe and beyond, with versions of the show appearing on Canadian, Swedish, Polish, Irish, Australian and North American television.

Within the boom in historical programming charted across Erin Bell and Ann Gray's edited collection, *Televising History*, *WDYTYA* is acknowledged to be 'extremely significant' (Bell and Gray 2010, p. 8). On British television it has been followed by a glut of programmes that have used family history research as an investigative narrative structure. These have included celebrity family history formats such as *Disappearing Britain* (Five, 2006), a three-part series produced by Testimony Films, in which a celebrity traces an aspect of social history intertwined with personal significance; *You Don't Know You're Born* (ITV1, 2007), produced by Wall to Wall, in which the personality experiences the lifestyle of their ancestor; and *Empire's Children* (Channel 4, 2007), also produced by Wall to Wall, a series which traces the effects and legacy of the Empire on six British celebrities.

There have also been reverse-celebrity family history formats: *My Famous Family* (UKTV History, 2007), in which Bill Oddie reveals some genealogical secrets to unsuspecting members of the public, and *So You Think You're Royal?* (Sky One, 2007–), a show which attempts to 'give British families, with claim to royal ancestry, the chance to retrace their heritage' (Thompson 2005). Non-celebrity family history programmes have included *Family Ties* (BBC4, 2004–6), which originally accompanied the broadcast of *WDYTYA*; *Not Forgotten* (Channel 4, 2005), a four-part series and one-off special, produced by Wall to Wall, which traced the descendants of First World War soldiers; *100% British* (Channel 4, 2006), another Wall to Wall production, a one-off documentary focused on genetic analysis in order to challenge the (nationalist) assumptions of its participants; and *The Last Slave* (Channel 4, 2007), a documentary commissioned to commemorate the 200th anniversary of Britain's abolition of the slave trade. It followed a Londoner as he traced back his family history to slave roots.[1] Family history has also arisen as a narrative and investigative form across daytime and lifestyle formats such as *History Mysteries* (BBC2, 2006), *Gene Detectives* (BBC1, 2007), *Heir Hunters* (BBC1, 2007–), parenting series *Never Did Me Any Harm* (Channel 4, 2007) and food show *A Taste of My Life* (BBC2, 2006).

Independent production company Wall to Wall was clearly able to initially capitalise on the winning formula of *WDYTYA* with a series of other related programmes, though none have enjoyed the sustained and international success of the 'original' format. So what has made *WDYTYA* such a significant and uniquely successful phenomenon? Billed by its producer Alex West as a mix of '*History Today* and *Heat*' (in Deans 2004), the series quickly came 'to symbolise the kind of programme the newly public service focused BBC should be doing: serious-minded, but also accessible and popular'.[2] Part of the programme's populist address lies in its use of celebrities, but can also be found in its focus on the desire to experience history at a personal and affective level, on the part of both the investigator and the audience. As such, *WDYTYA* clearly corresponds with recent trends in historical programming, which have been described by British historian and broadcaster Tristram Hunt as 'reality history'.[3] By placing the personal at the centre of understandings of public or social histories, the series uses family history and memory as a conduit between the past and present. Wall to Wall describes *WDYTYA* as a show which 'features famous names [...] as they venture on a journey of discovery into their ancestors' pasts to ultimately find out more about themselves, their family, and also our shared social history' (Wall to Wall press release, 2006). By remaining 'serious minded' and demanding personal stories which 'dovetail with big themes – Caribbean immigration, Indian Independence, World war, Industrial revolution' (Brown 2004), the programme-makers also weave the genealogical investigations of their various personalities, clearly chosen to offer a more encompassing vision of 'Britishness', into a potentially more inclusive history of Britain and British national identity.

The generic blending at work in *WDYTYA* along with its stress upon emotion and experience as modes of knowledge have been at the heart of its success in terms of circulating BBC promotional discourses. However, we might also relate these characteristics to the emphasis on memory within the series. Kerwin Klein writes that 'we sometimes use memory as a synonym for history to soften our prose, to humanize it, and make it more accessible. Memory simply sounds less distant, and perhaps for that reason, it often serves to help draw general readers into a sense of the relevance of history for their own lives' (2000, p. 129). Memory narratives in formats like *WDYTYA* might be viewed as a way of 'softening' social history documentary, employed as a populist strategy and as part of the increasing centrality of emotion in contemporary British television.

Whilst memory might be seen to allow a more emotional, 'softer' connection with history, it is the fluidity of memory, memory as a process, in a constant state of being made and unmade, that is significant for my own reading of the family history documentary. Alessandro Portelli has described memory as the 'permanent labour of connecting'.[4] The investigative narrative of *WDYTYA* foregrounds the labour of connecting in the work of genealogy – establishing and emphasising connections across the family tree. This form of labour also correlates with the acts of transfer involved in post-memorial work (Hirsch 1997; 2008) and the tracing of clues and fragments that characterise understandings of memory work (Kuhn 1995); each appears to fit the activities on display in the series and is discussed in more detail below. The labour of connecting also emphasises the role of construction, interpretation and imaginative investment in the acts of memory-making – where meaning is shaped by the needs and desires of the investigator, the programme-maker and wider cultural frames of remembrance.[5] However, the labour of connecting is immediately complicated by the *WDYTYA* investigators' tracing of a ready-made trail; this is, in a sense, memory work without the work – memory work which is performed and dramatised.

By focusing my analysis on some of its textual and narrative conventions, the trope of the 'journey' and the use of family photography, I want to consider how acts of memory-making are represented by the series. In the light of Myra Macdonald's work on television documentary conventions and how they can both enable and constrict memory work, I argue that the format simultaneously opens up a vision of a multicultural British heritage whilst closing down or 'taming' our relationships to difficult and contested areas of history and identity by the stress on an affirmative cultural citizenship. Here, the format reveals the ways in which remembering and forgetting are knitted together. Whilst the notion of the journey frames the formatted narrative, the international circulation of the format reveals the memorial obsessions, patterns of remembrance and televisual vernaculars of different television nations.

Emotional journeys

Helen Weinstein has spoken of how the 'emotional hook' provided by human interest stories has become central to the motivational and creative decision-making of television history producers.[6] It is important to acknowledge that the stress on emotion and experience, the blurring of 'hard' and soft' generic forms and the merging of private and public spheres form part of a wider trend in television programming that has been much discussed in television scholarship on the talk show (Shattuc 1997), factual programming (Bondebjerg 1996; Brunsdon et al. 2001) and reality television (Biressi and Nunn 2005), forms which have all clearly influenced *WDYTYA*.

Whilst these features are not new to the presentation of history on television, what is remarkable is the populist appeal of *WDYTYA* and the emotionalism and sensationalism inherent in its presentation and marketing. What these programmes exhibit is how, rather than viewing these categories as a marker of the 'dumbing down' of television, the elicitation of emotion, at least within BBC discourses, became the key to their value. It was the attention on the emotional revelations of comedian and presenter Bill Oddie and TV journalist Jeremy Paxman's stories and personalities that offered a point of media focus and promotion and opened the first and second series of *WDYTYA* respectively.[7] Rather than reading the interruption of the personal and the emotional and the incorporation of celebrities as, in Catherine Johnson's summary of the popular argument, part of the 'decline of factual programming and a concession to populism at the expense of the BBC's public service remit' (in Brunsdon et al. 2001, p. 41), generic blending becomes a point of renewal and success. In John Willis' speech at the Factual Forum on 18 March 2005, he remarked upon the qualities of *WDYTYA* among other recent BBC Two documentaries:

> Last month BBC2 had *Auschwitz, Tribe,* and *The Lost World of Mitchell and Kenyon,* riding high simultaneously. They were all very different, all attracted brilliant reviews and all surpassed expectation of audience size significantly. These programmes – and others like last autumn's hit from Wall to Wall – *Who Do You Think You Are?* – demonstrate that there is a clear audience appetite for traditional documentary virtues like strong narrative and genuine insight but illuminated in ways that feel modern and relevant, whether using celebrities or dramatic reconstruction.
>
> (Willis 2005)

Both celebrity and emotionality are central to the promotion of *WDYTYA* and are seen to function as a sign of the BBC's appeal to a more popular market, delivering programmes that are both 'serious' (traditional documentary virtues) and 'entertaining' (use of celebrities).

The incorporation of both celebrities and 'real people', the positioning of the celebrity as a 'real person', viewed at home with their families, and the programme's reliance upon personal memory and emotional revelation link the format with a series of recognisable television genres outside of historical programming – the confessional talk show, the celebrity talk show and, perhaps less obviously, the makeover show. Charlotte Brunsdon writes that the emphasis of contemporary lifestyle programmes is on 'what producers call "the reveal" [...] when the transformed person or place is shown to their nearest and dearest and the audience' (Brunsdon et al. 2001, p. 55). The moment of revelation is almost always coded as 'emotional' and 'melodramatic' through the use of the extreme close-up and the reaction shot. Paxman's seemingly uncharacteristic display of tears offers one particular example.[8]

Sitting alone in a plain room in a Bradford registry office, Paxman removes his glasses and is silent in response to the details of the death certificates of his ancestors. The camera quickly and jerkily zooms into an extreme close-up of the obviously 'choked-up' Paxman, as if desperate to record this glimpse of 'real' emotion. The moment of revelation is sustained by Paxman's repetition of the findings of the coroner's reports and a second display of emotionality where Paxman once again removes his glasses, as if revealing unseen layers of his 'personality', but then modestly partially covers his face with his hand from what feels like the prying gaze of the camera. Marking the setting of a precedent and the formulaic expectation of celebrity tears, the intrusive and lingering close-up that accompanies Paxman's 'breakdown' reveals its own strategy of manipulation. At this point the show's desperate attempts to elicit an emotional response from both Paxman and the viewer undermine its construction of that response as 'authentic'. However, the analytic gaze of the camera also highlights the role of the celebrity as both agent and subject of the investigation.

In his book *Cinematic Journeys*, Dimitris Eleftheriotis traces different types of movement and their relationship to a particular model of subjectivity that emerges in the nineteenth century – one which 'combines pleasure with the acquisition of knowledge, entertainment with self-improvement' (2010, p. 76). Investigating the representation of movements and journeys of exploration, discovery and revelation across a series of films, Eleftheriotis employs a conceptual dialectic of activity/passivity where the traveller is both 'an active observer and a "parcel", both explorer and explored'. He continues 'journeys not only lead to the discovery of startling new places and experiences but also propel towards self-discovery, as the travelling reveals new worlds and well-hidden emotions, memories or traumas, placing the traveller in a position of control over movement while being subjected to it' (2010, p. 77). Whilst the explorations of *WDYTYA* are of time and history as well as space, there is a corresponding view of the traveller as both 'explorer and explored'.

Framed within an investigative narrative structure, the celebrity embarks upon a physical and emotional journey. Whilst narratives of transformation and improvement pervade lifestyle television, *WDYTYA* attempts to encourage a reading of the journey to self-knowledge, both historical and emotional, as a means to self-improvement, charting how self-revelation leads to self-awareness.[9] The show's therapeutic aspects in its employment of a form of post-memory work are beneficial for some of its celebrity participants, as Bill Oddie states, 'this isn't curiosity, this journey – it's self-help', whilst others, though spectacularly revealed as an emotional being are more resistant to the prescribed reading: as Jeremy Paxman comments – 'What did I learn from the delving into my family background? I got a strong impression that the producer wanted me to say the experience had somehow changed my life. It didn't' (Paxman 2006, p. 19).

Mark Lawson commented in *The Guardian* that *WDYTYA* has 'the feel of a version of Great Railway Journeys in which the geography is personal' (Lawson 2004). It is perhaps the trope of the journey that is the most significant for the show. Whilst the format charts the mundane aspects of the quests of its investigators – the physical journeying across the country and even the globe in some episodes, the arrival at libraries and archives, and the negotiation of the dusty corridors of history – the journey in *WDYTYA* is also meant to be read as having a metaphorical significance. It is meant to be read as an emotional journey of self-discovery. As actress and novelist Meera Syal comments at the end of her journey in India: 'Even if you only go back one generation, you will experience a lot just on the journey.'[10]

In the first episode of the first series of *WDYTYA*,[11] Bill Oddie's investigations into his family history focused on the story of his mother, Lillian. Suffering from severe mental illness, Lillian was hospitalised during Oddie's childhood and remained in an institution for the majority of her life. Knowing little of his mother's history, and remembering less, it is the family photograph which is presented as a source of anxiety for Oddie, and prompts his search for personal meaning and memory. It is significant that it is in the representation of journeying and the beginning of Oddie's investigations that the four images that Oddie has of his mother are inserted into the documentary, where the view of a grey Birmingham suburb from inside a moving car is interrupted by the black-and-white image of the young Oddie with his mother, fragmented from its context so as to focus on this relationship and sliding into the frame from right to left. The movement into the frame is accompanied by a familiar 'rushing' sound as when two cars pass each other. Placed against the travelling shot, the movement of the image into the frame and the accompanying noise give the impression that the image forms another part of the landscape/cityscape viewed from the car; that in this case the geography has literally become personal. This image is followed by another three photographs of Oddie's mother; the quality, colouring and composition of the images clearly mark them as amateur family photographs but also place them into a biographical timescale. The family album is perhaps a practice of photographical collection and exhibition that many of us recognise, and it attaches an image-narrative to our personal memories. What is interesting in Oddie's case, revealed through both the dialogue and the presentation of these few images, is that Oddie's own sparse family album is seen to reflect his own lack of memory or knowledge in relation to his mother and his mother's story. For Oddie, the lack of narrative meaning is a cause of anxiety, unrest and the drive for meaning. Oddie's own mental health problems are disclosed at the start of the programme, and Oddie himself speculates that his relationship with his mother might lie at the root of his depression. One might argue that this anxiety, the lack of and desire for understanding or 'closure' is revealed in the presentation and movement of the photographs in the sequence, allowing us to position the significance of the images for Oddie and the documentary in relation to a therapeutic discourse.

The effect of the zoom into the image accompanied by the switch of image which pulls back each time to an increased length of the shot scale gives the impression of an object that although one might be moving towards it is continually out of reach. This effect is heightened by the alternating movement of the images, the first sliding into the frame from the right to the left, a movement that reverses with each new image, and the repetition of the piano riff on the soundtrack, which emphasises the sense of continuity without climax or conclusion.

It is important to note that this sequence doesn't stress Lillian's experience, locked within the images, but Oddie's experience of these photographs; what is revealed in the dialogue is how they become his memory of the photographs rather than them being photographs of a memory. As Oddie himself remarks: 'When I look back at my childhood, I have about four images which involve my mother. They are like a scene out of a movie, y' know, they're like here's the best of... this is the trailer as it were. But I never did see the film.' The enigma photograph, the image without a clear indexical link, is often central to the investigative drive of *WDYTYA*. As a documentary format that functions as both an investigation of aspects of our social history and as narratives of self-discovery, the image of a national landscape is built up via the personal and the emotional. This point is revealed in this sequence by the interruption of a personal geography into the frame.

Dramatising the family archive

In the family history documentary the presentation of family photography is a key textual and narrative strategy. Family photographs function as a conduit, allowing an intersection with wider historical narratives and acting as an anchor, connecting the viewer to the subject of the investigations. In *WDYTYA*, family photographs offer the first port of call in the celebrity's journey, a journey which is structured, via their use, as both an investigative and an emotional one. A visit to a parent or elderly relative often facilitates the introduction of the images, which will recur throughout the programme, revealing the celebrity's connection to the subjects of investigation and any details that remain within living memory. The photographs immediately begin to take on two functions in the documentary: as a source of evidence along with the presentation of other historical documents located in various archives (letters, reports, birth/death certificates) validating oral accounts of memory and history, and as a point of emotional connection between the investigator and the subject of his or her investigations and where the viewer, via various presentational strategies, is pulled into this connection.

Marianne Hirsch's influential concept of 'postmemory' is useful, not only in relation to the 'intergenerational acts of transfer' (2008, p. 106) exhibited in a format such as *WDYTYA*, but also in the programme's reliance on family photography for its forms of storytelling. Hirsch writes of postmemory's connection to the past as being mediated via 'imaginative investment, projection and creation' rather than recall. It is a connection that can be both familial and affiliative as she suggests how post-memorial work

> strives to *reactivate* and *reembody* more distant social/national and archival/cultural memorial structures by reinvesting them with resonant and individual and familial forms of mediation and aesthetic expression. Thus less-directly affected participants can become engaged in the generation of postmemory, which can thus persist even after all participants and even their familial descendants are gone.
>
> (Emphasis in original, 2008, p. 111)

The resonance of such familial images and narratives, pervasive in their use within public memorial sites, is predicated upon the 'power of the *idea* of family' and the 'forms of mutual *recognition* that define family images and narratives' (emphasis in original, 2008, p. 113). Whilst photographs open up a series of potential emotional engagements and imaginative investments between the subject and the archive, these forms of mutual recognition also point towards shared practices of memory and remembrance that arguably interject the viewer into the programme's strategies of historical investigation and memory-making.

What interests me here are the various ways in which the archive, in particular the family's photographic archive, is animated or dramatised in the service of the investigator's experiences, needs and desires, and the storytelling strategies of the programme-makers.[12] For example, the presentation of what we might refer to as 'enigma photographs' is often key to the investigations in *WDYTYA* where the absence of memory or knowledge in relation to an existing archive of images acts as a narrative drive. This investigative strategy is employed, for example, in actress Shelia Hancock's episode in series two of *WDYTYA* as she seeks to establish the identity of a charismatic and wealthy woman pictured in a photograph from her family collection.[13] Similar to the 'magical value' of the photograph famously written about by Walter Benjamin and his encounter with a nineteenth-century image of a Newhaven fishwife producing an 'unruly desire to know what her name was, the women who was alive then' (1999, p. 510), Hancock articulates a lifelong desire to find out the identity of the woman.

The narrative framing of photographic mysteries is inevitably heightened by the presentation of the photographs, their plotting within the tale, the layering of voice and image and, as highlighted in the earlier analysis of Oddie's episode, the use of movement. Karen Lury has written evocatively about the contemplative opportunities of the rostrum camera effect and how 'the frequent use of the rostrum camera mobilises the still photographic image so that the point of view moves around the image, 'seeking out' something – though what this is, exactly, may not be entirely clear' (2003, p. 103). This seems to respond to the illusion of experience captured that photography evokes,[14] where, to quote Marita Sturken, 'memory appears to reside within the photographic image, to tell its story in response to our gaze' (1997, p. 19). Whilst reacting to the seeming need to present a moving image, the movement to close-up articulates the desire to 'seek-out' the 'truth' of the image and a greater knowledge of its subject. The plotting and repetition of particular images across the investigative narrative dramatises that illusion of knowledge sought and gained.

Episode ten of the sixth series of *WDYTYA* sees actress Kim Cattrall's investigation of her missing grandfather, George Baugh, who abandoned his wife and three daughters in 1949.[15] Whilst the episode breaks with the now well-established structure of the format to focus on one particular story, its presentation of photographs illuminates their performative function within the series. Visiting her mother and aunts in Liverpool, Cattrall is presented with a tattered and yellowing photograph of a wedding scene from 1934. In it, the family is arranged on the pavement outside a double-fronted Victorian house. Pointed out by her aunt, a cut to close-up reveals the mysterious George Baugh peering out from behind a net curtain at the corner of the right bay window, and the women speculate as to why he wouldn't want to be photographed.

The image appears twice again, plotted at particular points in Cattrall's investigation. After her initial family visit she reflects on George's character. The image is inserted into Cattrall's reflections and the rostrum camera's move to a close-up of the young man peering out of the window accompanies her questioning of his actions: why he did what he did and 'what went through his head?' The photograph is used for a third time and presented in the same way following the revelation that George had stowed away on a ship bound for America in 1948. Absent for a month he eventually returned to his wife and fathered a third daughter. Cattrall remarks: 'I'm piecing together a man who doesn't have a tremendous amount of responsibility except to his own desires and needs.' The shady image of a man who is interpreted as refusing to join the wedding party is employed on these occasions to signify, in the first instance, the mysteriousness of George's character and, in the second, the increasing selfishness of his actions. The revelation of his bigamous second marriage quickly follows.

Pictures remain at the forefront of Cattrall's quest. Travelling to meet a relative of George's second wife Isabel, she comments: 'I'm really hoping for a picture. I'm hoping to find something in his face which is about regret or remorse, because I would like to think leaving those three girls behind – there was a consequence to that.' Encountering a series of family snaps instead – a sunny beach holiday, portraits of suburban affluence following the new Baugh family's emigration to Australia – they only serve to confirm Cattrall's suspicions as to his heartless character: 'this doesn't look like a man who really spends any time thinking about the past. He's just living right in that moment and not looking back.'

The story of George Baugh and his character as a man are constructed predominantly through the 'reading' of a series of photographs: the sunny family snaps which cannot help but be read against the episode's opening use of a gloomy black-and-white photograph of Kim's grandmother Marian stood in the yard of a back-to-back terrace, smiling in a woolly hat, gloves and coat buttoned up to her neck. The latter image is contextualised by the archive film of poverty and unemployment in pre-Second World War Liverpool and the poignant memories of hardship endured by Marian and her daughters. The contrast in lifestyles only serves to reaffirm the anger felt by Cattrall, her mother and her aunts.

The forms of 'imaginative investment, projection and creation' that are at work in relation to the episode's use of a family archive are amplified by tensions that exist within the format and its use of celebrities. As with the Paxman example, *WDYTYA*, whilst seeking to uncover a personality's 'authentic self' (predominantly through displays of tearful emotion), walks a fine line between a spontaneous response to the revelations of the archive and the management of that response by both the programme-makers, who lay the trail for the celebrity to follow, and the status of the celebrity as a 'professional performer'. The tension inherent in the latter becomes most clear in the encounters between the celebrity and the 'ordinary' person and has implications for the forms of memory and remembering constructed by the programme. For example, Cattrall is strikingly different from the *Sex and the City* (HBO, 1998–2004) character she is famous for playing. Whilst Samantha Jones is bold, brash and hyper-confident, Cattrall has a much softer voice, she is poised and graceful, gentle and respectful. Internationally successful, she is also much closer to a Hollywood level of fame than the more parochial BBC television personalities that commonly feature within the series. As a professional actress, her comfort in front of the cameras is contrasted by the initial uneasiness of the family members she meets. It allows her a certain authority which effectively manages the memories and stories that are shared. The elderly Maisy and her daughter Shelia, relations of Isabel Baugh, are in constant agreement with the interpretations that Cattrall makes. Initially describing George as a good family man, a 'nice' uncle, Cattrall's bitter response to the revelation of his emigration to Australia, which she interprets as yet another 'brazen' act of selfishness, tearing his heartbroken second wife from her family, is met by another series of agreements. From describing George's actions as shockingly against character, Maisy's voice trembles as she recalls the family's tearful separation from Isabel, and George is re-remembered in a different light, as selfishly breaking up her own family as well.

I am not claiming here that Cattrall is consciously manipulating the memories being shared but that the effect of her own authority as celebrity and professional performer – Maisy remarks that it has been a privilege to meet her and as the 'interview' ends she visibly relaxes and sweetly offers her a cup of tea – and her understandably biased reading of George's character and life story inevitably impact on the processes of remembering and the interpretation of the family archive. This is then reproduced and reaffirmed in Cattrall's repetition of George's story on her return to see her mother and aunts. Here Cattrall returns as family curator, telling the story through the images she has collected. With a conscious sense of timing and dramatic effect the photographs she hands over are accompanied by a series of prefaces and pauses, allowing her family the time to react to each one.

The performances on display in *WDYTYA* and the central role of family photographs reveal much about the imaginative investments that are made in the encounter with the family archive and the kinds of stories that are spun from it. In some ways Cattrall's episode is unique in its focus on one particular family mystery but the features of the tale illuminate some of the strategies and tensions within the format with regards to reality television's 'desire to dramatise' (see Piper 2004, p. 274) – a desire which might be seen to correlate with Martin Saar's discussion of genealogy as a rhetorical-narrative tool. Saar argues that genealogies 'take their critical force from the dramatising gesture', constructing stories around 'paradigmatic moments' and producing a vision of 'broad historical lines and developments' (2002, p. 329).

Connecting the celebrity to these 'broad historical lines', the written archival document is also both a source of evidence and a point of emotional connection. The 'official' evidence of the written word itself often prompts an emotional response. Paxman's reading of his ancestor's death certificate, Stephen Fry's opening of a document detailing the fates of his relations and the horror of the word 'Auschwitz',[16] Moira Stuart's handling of the records of slave ownership and the listed names of the enslaved[17] – each is a moment which breaks the composure of the celebrity. Similar to the rostrum camera's 'poring over' of the photographic image, the evidence of names and dates uncovered in historical documents is also often presented via a move to close-up. A different form of imaginative investment is at work here – one which emphasises the historical aura of the document and its evidentiary power – closer to Derrida's 'archive fever' than the 'magical value' of the photograph. These emotional encounters with the archive illuminate the significance, within the series, on the physical sites of memory, and point towards other forms of encounter with the materials of memory.

Empty space and memory work

The investigative activities of the television personalities in *WDYTYA*, the piecing together of the puzzles presented to them, might be seen to correlate with Annette Kuhn's delineation of 'memory work'. She writes in *Family Secrets* that:

> The past is gone forever. We cannot return to it, nor can we reclaim it now as it was. But that does not mean it is lost to us. The past is like the scene of a crime: if the deed itself is irrecoverable, its traces may still remain [...] Memory work has a great deal in common with

forms of inquiry which – like detective work and archaeology, say – involve working backwards – searching for clues, deciphering signs and traces, making deductions, patching together reconstructions out of fragments of evidence.

(1995, p. 4)

The investigative strategies of 'memory work' are clearly reminiscent of the practices of genealogy and the lines of inquiry the celebrities journey down. As part of this journeying the show places a great deal of emphasis upon *sites* of memory that are significant for the investigators' family narratives. It is an emphasis that illuminates the potential for the interaction between place and memory within this particular television documentary format.

In Myra Macdonald's study of the 'performance of memory' in a series of documentaries from the 1990s that focus on the 1960s, she analyses how television documentary conventions both vivify and constrict memory work. For Macdonald, drawing on Kuhn, the 'specificity of place' has the potential to act as a 'powerful stimulus of memory' (2006, p. 336). However, in Macdonald's examples, 'by routinely filming interviewees against interior backdrops that lack precise indices of cultural or geographical context', the documentaries 'miss opportunities to experiment with the interactions between place and memory' (2006, p. 336). *WDYTYA*, however, places an emphasis on the idea of origin and belonging, and stresses the attachment between place and memory, though the memory workers of *WDYTYA* are often faced with the empty spaces and weeds of memory and history. A desire for a sense of continuity between past and present is often expressed by the celebrity investigator and indeed by the family history documentary itself; a desire to see, through ancestral connections, how we got to where we are today. The history of the identity formation of both the self and the nation is fundamental to the project of the family history documentary.

Developing an increased understanding of the self through an investigation of personal memory and history invariably overlaps with various therapeutic discourses, including practices of memory work and phototherapy. Meanwhile, the 're-imagining' of the nation and the importance of understanding the historical continuity of national identity overlaps with other accounts of British history and identity, illustrated by Simon Schama's *A History of Britain* (BBC, 2000–2) – 'it's only when we know what we have been that we can begin to understand our place in the scheme of things, to discover as a nation who we are'.[18] We must therefore understand the importance of the oscillation between the personal and social in the family history documentary as accompanied by a similar movement between the past and the present, but one which is inhabited by a strong desire for a sense of continuity for historical meaning to have contemporary significance.

This, however, is often complicated by the fact that, as Kuhn states, 'the past is gone forever' and there is often nothing to see. History, by definition, has gone. What we are left with is the search for presence in absence. Perhaps it is an aesthetic of absence that might more broadly characterise history on television, as Simon Schama notes – 'we are in the business of representing something that is no longer there' (cited in Champion 2003, p. 116). For example, comedian David Baddiel's attempts to locate the site of his grandfather's brick factory in Poland are met by the encounter with a landscape which is, according to the comedian, 'as bleak as it gets'.[19] As he surveys two crumbling and graffitied brick stacks on a grey, rain-beaten and flooded scrubland, he remarks upon his disappointment that being on a programme which is about getting *in touch* with the past, the past he encounters has been 'blown out of existence'.

The problem of the absences of history is partly resolved by what we might refer to as an 'iconography of memory'; graves, ruins, memorials, weeds. TV presenter Jeremy Clarkson responds to the absence of history at the site of his ancestors' former glassworks that most of industrial history is now '*just weeds*'.[20] Kerwin Klein writes that 'such memorial tropes have emerged as one of the common features of our new cultural history where in monograph after monograph, readers confront the abject object: photographs are torn, mementos faded, toys broken' (2000, p. 136). Television, however, is left with the problem of filling this empty space. There are various strategies, detailed by several of the contributors to Roberts and Taylor's collection *The Historian, Television and Television History* (2001), to overcoming the dominance of this absence, through the appeal of storytelling and to the imagination. However, I want to suggest that this empty space is key to the representation of memory and significant for the emotional pull of a programme like *WDYTYA*.

Significantly, for the programme, a photographic archive is no longer enough in terms of evidence; this perhaps reflects a desire for unmediated experience which necessitates a return to the sites of memory and the origin of the specific photograph. However, our investigators are often met with absence, and the empty spaces they encounter often resonate with the knowledge that something was once there. This is often achieved by the use of image matches, between the 'then' of the photograph and the 'now' of the investigations. This strategy, similar to the photographic practice of 'rephotography', is employed to encourage a direct comparison between the then and the now, to offer an examination of how things have changed, where empty space resonates with the knowledge that something meaningful was once there, and to validate the existence of that something meaningful.

In an example from Ian Hislop's episode of *WDYTYA*,[21] he visits the site of a Boer War battle in which his grandfather fought. The events of the battle, including the massive casualties sustained by the British army, are related by the battle historian who accompanies Hislop. At this point, a photograph depicting a trench of bodies, killed in the battle, is matched against the image of the grave as it is today (see Figure 3.1). The shot scale and camera position of the original image are reproduced so the content of the 'then' is transposed onto the image of the 'now', revealing what horrors lie in the quiet and sunny grave. In Jeremy Clarkson's episode, he returns to the town where his ancestors, the Kilners, had their first glass factory. We cut from a long shot taken from the hill overlooking a northern town, a square of houses outlining a large field in the centre of the frame where the factory would have been, to a nineteenth-century illustration of the factory, held in front of the camera by Clarkson, who exclaims as the scene progresses, that such a huge factory is 'just sports pitches now' (see Figure 3.2). By matching the images of the 'now' and 'then' in the centre of the frame, through this juxtaposition we are invited to read into the significance of the comparison as the ghosts of both Clarkson's and Britain's industrial heritage echo in the space of the frame.

The fear of the loss of historical and personal significance is also illuminated by Bill Oddie as he returns to the psychiatric hospital where his mother was treated, only to find it has been redeveloped as an executive housing estate: 'thus are memories totally obliterated'. Once again the viewer is offered a comparison between the now and the then through the use of an image match, reproducing shot scale and camera position, as a photograph of the front of the hospital in the 1950s is juxtaposed against an image of the site today.

Image matches are not always used to highlight the more disruptive or erosive examples of historical change but to stress the sense of continuity, particularly in the relationship between the investigators and their ancestors. The desire for a continuum is continually stressed by the revisiting of significant ancestral sites and the retracing of ancestral steps in the search for memory and historical significance.

The evidentiary quality of the photograph enables the investigator to trace the site of memory and place themselves in the position of the

Figure 3.1 Then and now: The battle grave (*WDYTYA*, series 1, episode 5, Wall to Wall for BBC, 2004).

subject of the photograph. For example, on her return to her great, great-grandfather's hometown in South Yorkshire, opera singer Lesley Garrett seeks out the site where the photograph she has of him was taken.[22] The family's butchers' business is now a greengrocer, but the crumbling yard wall, in front of which the photograph was taken, is still there. Garrett holds the photograph up, comparing the image against its remains in order to confirm the location. She then positions herself in the place where her ancestor stood in the image ('so me granddad would

Figure 3.2 Jeremy Clarkson surveys the former site of the Kilner factory (*WDYTYA*, series 1, episode 4, Wall to Wall for BBC, 2004).

'av been stood about 'ere, looking out, that's amazing!'). The medium-long shot of Garrett standing in the empty yard, in the place of her grandfather, then cuts to a close-up of Garrett's hand holding the late nineteenth-century photograph of the butcher stood in his yard. The physical alignment of investigator and ancestor encourages the sense of continuity, enabling the development of an empathetic connection as well.

There are examples in *WDYTYA* where the recreation of the content of the photographic image is used to forge a link between past and present, immediate and ancestral family relations. In Stephen Fry's episode, he returns with his mother to her childhood home and the pair explore the present-day garden, searching for the locations of the photographs they have and then setting up lines of continuity rather than rupture between the then and now. In one example, with the camera positioned behind Fry and his mother, he holds up the black-and-white image of her and her sisters as children positioned on the garden steps and sat on a stone urn. The photograph is held up by Fry in the centre of the frame and is matched against the lines of the steps and the edge of the garden (see Figure 3.3). The lush green of the present-day garden almost seamlessly merges into the black-and-white tones of the photograph, and it is almost as if we are peering across time, through the centre of the image and into the past. Rather than juxtaposing the images of past and present, preferring to have them exist and blend in the same frame establishes a strong sense of continuity.

As the scene progresses, Fry and his mother reproduce the subject positions of another family image of her and her father stood in front of the house ('so you were standing just there and in fact if we go round we could reproduce it'), with Fry taking the place of his grandfather (which, he quips, is a 'Freudian nightmare') and his mother placed back in her childhood position, standing in front of Fry. Fry then holds the

Figure 3.3 Peering through time: Fry and his mother retrace old steps (*WDYTYA*, series 2, episode 3, Wall to Wall for BBC, 2006).

photograph in front of the pair to confirm the match for the cameras, once again stressing continuity rather than juxtaposition by placing the investigator where the ancestor was pictured. The attachment to a site of memory arguably encourages a sense of belonging which reaffirms the investigators' search for their place in history.

Empty space does not always need photographic imagery in order to create a sense of resonance; it is often filled with oral testimonies of memory which can achieve a similar effect via the empathetic response and imaginative investment of the viewer. For example, having returned to his childhood home in the suburbs of Birmingham, Oddie wanders around the space inside; he recalls his time spent there and observes how the space has and hasn't changed. Oddie moves up to the first floor and reaches the bathroom at the top of the stairs; it is here that he recounts a particular memory he has of his mother. As Oddie describes the memory of walking in on his mother in the bath, how she was unfamiliar to him and how unfazed she was by the interruption, he stares into the bath and tugs his beard as he recalls the experience whilst focusing on the site of his memory. We then cut to a shot that pans across the length of the empty bath and lingers on the image as if a similar focus could recall the experience on the part of the viewer. What we are being asked to do is to imaginatively invest the story into the image, to appreciate this empty yet ordinary space as the site of a profoundly personal experience, to witness the resonance of memory.

Absences within the various official archives also generate forms of resonance that are poignant reminders of official attempts at the making and unmaking of memory. In the Holocaust narratives of Stephen Fry and David Baddiel, whereas the fates of Fry's relatives are revealed by the historical records, the fate of Baddiel's great uncle Arno, assumed to have perished in the Warsaw Ghetto, remains uncorroborated by the absence of his name in any records. Moira Stuart's journey to Dominica leads her to the official records of nineteenth-century slave owners where the enslaved are listed only by their newly given Christian names – the erasure of their original names and surnames precluding further ancestral investigation and leaving the trail cold. Here an aesthetic of absence has a relational link to historical and political campaigns of erasure.

The emphasis on place and the retracing of ancestral steps appear as a form of re-enactment that link the format with other trends in historical programming (see Agnew 2007) including the popularity of the 'historical travelogue'. Recent years have seen presenters such as Julia Bradbury and Nicholas Crane retracing the paths of famous travel writers in *Wainwright Walks* (BBC, 2007–), *Great British Journeys* (BBC, 2007) and *Nicholas Crane's Britannia* (BBC, 2009).[23] The spectacle of landscape and a strong heritage discourse serve to emphasise lines of tradition that feed into constructions of national identity and 'Britishness'. In *WDYTYA*, with its emphasis on personal identity and transformation, the interplay between the individual and the collective is embedded, once again, through the trope of the journey. Here we might return to Eleftheriotis' work on cinematic journeys, as his argument aligns with the genealogical explorations of the family history format:

> such explorations and the movements that enable them are not only quests for pleasure but also for meaning, as the mobile subject often retraces tracks already laid out and finds him/herself travelling journeys that include but also exceed individuals, the journeys of the anonymous collective subjects of grand narratives.
>
> (2010, p. 32)

Following a trail laid by the programme-makers but also retracing the tracks of ancestors and the 'journeys of the anonymous collective subjects of grand narratives' *WDYTYA* as family *and* social history documentary is invested in building a particular portrait of the nation, inevitably shaped by the stories the producers choose to tell.

Closed space? Home and nation

The domestic lives of the celebrity investigators and their interactions with family and friends are often featured in *WDYTYA*. Our celebrities are often positioned at home at both the beginning and end of their respective journeys, often returning to their families with the information, images and even relics or mementoes they've gathered on their family histories. Meera Syal returns from tracing her grandfather's story in India to her parent's home in Epping Forest with a brick taken from her mother's family home. Stephen Fry returns to a family gathering to reveal the fates of the related Lamm family who were discovered to have perished at Auschwitz. Actress Amanda Redman's journey also concludes with a family gathering, though this time it is more celebratory, as she introduces some long-lost cousins to the family.[24] Lesley Garrett is viewed returning from Yorkshire to her London home and an enthusiastic reception from her children, whilst David Baddiel returns home to his mother and daughter to celebrate his fortieth birthday. In Jeremy Paxman's episode, the return to familiar surroundings, and arguably to his more familiar television personality, is marked by his return to the *Newsnight* (BBC, 1980–) studio, whilst Moira Stuart returns from the lapping shores of the Caribbean to the River Thames and the familiar cityscape of the London embankment.

The cyclical nature of these journey narratives and the insistence on the return home or at least to familiar surroundings and iconography seems suggestive of, contrary to the aesthetic of empty space, a way of closing down imaginative investment. Memory work as process, as the 'permanent labour of connecting', is illuminated by the trope of the journey, but an insistence on affirmation and a stress on completion and closure is emphasised in the denouement of the various stories. The loss of family members and ancestors is often filled by the discovery of distant relations and new familial connections. For example, whilst David Baddiel is unable to ascertain the fate of his uncle, he encounters new, albeit distantly related, family members in London's Jewish community. In Macdonald's analysis of the codes and conventions of television documentary that 'act both to vivify but also to constrict "memory work"' (2006, p. 327), she concludes that 'television too often finds ways to integrate, and subdue, the performance of witnesses' memories within its own narrative and visual requirements. Commentary and archive footage, with their directing or generalising capacities, tend to smooth away the rough edges of potential moments of disruption or tension in memory evocation' (2006, p. 342). The return to the safety of the home is suggestive of one of the ways in which television is often involved in a process of 'taming' difficult material.

WDYTYA has undoubtedly been successful in its campaign objectives, prompting through a multi-platform approach an increase in the genealogical enquiries of the British public.[25] Whilst the format was designed to 'dovetail' with larger themes and histories, it arguably creates a more inclusive and affirmative vision of a British national identity. The content of the histories represented in *WDYTYA* might be seen as a negotiation with, for example, Britain's post-colonial identity reflected in the selection of television personalities such as Meera Syal, Moira Stuart, athlete Colin Jackson and TV chef Ainsley Harriot. An image of a 'New Britain' is arguably realised through the personal narratives of emotion and experience charting social, industrial, colonial and wartime family histories. Writing on the theme of 'relational movement', in which different types of mobility are placed in 'comparative frames of reference' (2010, p. 125), Eleftheriotis sensitively illuminates a 'process of cultural syncretism' within which 'journeys of exploration, discovery and revelation are substantially contextualised by movements of displacement, exile, diaspora and migration' (2010, p. 124). However, where the experiences of dispossession and dislocation, often as a result of the movements of the British Empire, are uncovered by the celebrity investigators, the tales of the colonised, via acts of transfer and post-memorial work are, more often than not, appropriated back into a multicultural narrative of New Britain. For example, quintessentially English actor Rupert Penry-Jones' journey to India uncovers a colonial family line which goes back eight generations. However, the history he pursues is whether or not he has Indian ancestry and a personal multicultural heritage, rather than challenging the legacy of colonial power in mixed race relationships.[26]

Whilst in some ways the programme opens up a productive engagement with personal and national history and memory, there is an overemphasis on catharsis and closure – the end point of the therapeutic narrative – which closes down further investigation into the more difficult stories. Aside from the risk of appropriation, the affirmations and melodramatic gestures of the format might be seen to preclude further investigation into these difficult histories, whilst returning us to the insistence on the traumatic and painful content of memory and history. The dramatising gestures, the stress on emotional engagement and experiential knowledge all, according to Helen Weinstein, are effective ways of delivering audiences for 'UK TV history products' to broadcasters. But these must be situated within wider concerns surrounding a 'contemporary confessional culture in which the key attraction is the disclosure of true emotions' (Aslama and Pantti 2006, p. 167). In some senses, the family history documentary may suffer from an emptying out of meaning, replaced by the fascination with celebrity revelations or with the private genealogical investigations of the viewer.[27] We might also question whether certain forms of televisual memory re-engage audiences with their private and emotional engagements with memory and history at the cost of the exorcism of the irreconcilable and the problematic, returning us to familiar patterns of collective remembering and forgetting. This dialectic informs Paul Gilroy's conceptualisation of 'post-imperial melancholia', where British culture's 'unhealthy' obsession with both world wars (embodied in the football chant 'Two world wars and one World Cup') and specifically the conflict with Nazi Germany is obsessively re-imagined whilst there is the absence of other colonial conflicts in popular cultural memory.[28] This patterned and pathological forgetting of our colonial past and its continued impact on

British society today is positioned against the overabundance of other kinds of dominant memory.[29]

Travelling television

Emerging over the last few years as a global brand, *WDYTYA*'s formatted approach to representations of the past inevitably promotes the forms of storytelling encouraged by the genealogical narrative – the emphasis on emotional engagement and the dovetailing of grand narratives with personal stories. Television memory canons are inevitably weighted according to national contexts and are particularly significant for certain understandings of national identity – the dynamics of remembering and forgetting are endemic in the stories each nation tells of itself. For example, produced in the period of the family history television boom, the awkwardly titled series *Where Was Your Family During the Famine?* (RTE, 2008) used genealogy to investigate a key moment in *Irish* history. Whilst the British family history documentary predominantly engages with tales of industry, empire and world war, the American version has a different canon of historical events that are dovetailed with the celebrity's ancestral line – the foundational myths of puritan fundamentalism, European colonialism and immigration, the American Civil War and the legacy of slavery. Indeed the latter is central to the celebrated genealogical series *African American Lives* (PBS, 2006–8), a miniseries hosted by Harvard historian Henry Louis Gates, Jr. that focused on the family histories of prominent African Americans explored through genealogy and genetic analysis.

The *WDYTYA* format's movement between different television nations offers an additional form of relational movement to be investigated in this chapter. In Albert Moran's essay on programme formats and international and domestic television cultures, he usefully highlights how circulating formats become 'modified to seem local or national in origin', acting as a 'flexible template or empty mould awaiting particular social inflexion and accent in other television territories to appeal to home audiences in that place' (2009, p. 151). The most immediate version of such modification is apparent in the different national adaptations of the *WDYTYA* brand image – originally featuring the simple image of a lush green tree mounted on a grassy hill and framed against a blue sky, an image which neatly symbolises the dynamic of the individual (the lone tree) and the collective (the genealogical map) at the heart of the format's historical project (see Figure 3.4). Whilst each version keeps the title graphics the same (a plain sans serif font in white framed

Figure 3.4   *WDYTYA's* original brand image (Wall to Wall for BBC, 2004–).

by the connective lines of the family tree structure) and employs a similar composition, the features and colours of the natural landscape vary. The Australian version (SBS One, 2007–) features a scorched-looking tree against a royal azure blue sky and burnt orange grassland. The Canadian adaptation (CBC, 2007) employs an autumnal-coloured maple tree against a sunny jade sky dotted with white clouds, and a flock of geese flying in the distance against a light blue mountain range. The Irish version (RTE1, 2008–) modifies the image to produce an emerald green tree atop a similar coloured hill, a line of grey hills in the distance and rays of sunlight bursting through a dark rain-clouded sky. Each image is clearly adapted to reflect the differing and iconic landscapes of the different nations, with shifts in colour and shape – the emerald green, the maple tree – signifying a new territory open to genealogical investigation. Whilst further pointing towards the connections between landscape and national identity, the shifting brand images are also a clear example of the global format as a 'flexible template' that can be invested with national specificities. This is further compounded by the specificity of the format and its explicit address to questions of national histories and identities.

Despite Moran's assertion that the advent of television formats can be seen to signal the 'emphatic endurance or even reappearance' (2009, p. 157) of the national within a new *television* landscape, the circulation of such templates has implications for what Sonja de Leeuw, through Anthony Giddens, refers to as the 'global creation of a standardised past' (2010, p. 142), with each version open to the critiques of the British series – its taming of difficult histories and the overemphasis on celebrity revelations. However, it is the differences that I want to focus on here; to explore how the grammar and accent of different television nations might be revealed through comparative versions of the travelling format.

Co-produced by Wall to Wall and Is or Isn't Entertainment (the production company of *Friends* actress Lisa Kudrow), the first series of the US version of *WDYTYA* was broadcast by NBC in March 2010. In the World Cup summer of the same year three episodes of this series, featuring Sarah Jessica Parker, Brooke Shields and Susan Sarandon, were transmitted on BBC One, scheduled as an alternative to the football coverage. Travelling from the UK to the US and back again is not a unique journey in terms of the circulation of television formats, with the American versions of reality TV hits such as *Wife Swap* (ABC/Channel 4, 2004–) or *Hell's Kitchen* (Fox/ITV, 2005–) often being brought back to their UK channel of origin with the expectation that they will be 'louder and brasher than the originals' (Sutcliffe, 2010). What is interesting in the case of the imported version of *WDYTYA* is how it was re-edited and re-modified for the British audience. Taking the US and the UK broadcasts of Sarah Jessica Parker's episode as the example, I want to consider the stylistic shifts in the format which produce a series of changes in the tone and address of the show.

The US series debuted on 5 March 2010 with actress Sarah Jessica Parker's exploration of her family history. Investigating her mother's 'German' side of the family tree, Parker firmly believes herself to be of immigrant stock, referring to herself as a 'mutt' (though this reference is absent from the US version). She encounters, however, a new identity as an 'archetypal American' as her ancestors are revealed to have been involved in key events in American history – the 1849 Gold Rush and the Salem witch trials of 1692. She proudly proclaims: 'I have real stock in this country, real roots...you know, I'm an American, I'm actually an American.' The format remains heavily invested in the construction of national identities though on this occasion it is the dubious uncovering of an archetypal/authentic American identity as Parker's family line collides with these 'foundational' moments.

The NBC version, classified as 'alternative reality' by the US television industry, has a much faster pace than the original British format, which producer Lisa Kudrow acknowledges as being a result of the US series being bought by NBC.[30] Lasting 40 minutes and totalling one hour with commercials, there is less time for historical context and an *increased* emphasis on the 'personal emotional journey' of the celebrity.

This is achieved by the heavy use of 'sentimental' musical layovers, the celebrity's own voice-over narration of the journey in first person, and a closing montage framed by a pop track (*Little Wonders* by Rob Thomas), which acts both as a musical coda and self-consciously works to memorialise the journey.

The BBC reversioning is extended to an uninterrupted 45-minute programme; the removal of commercials also sees the removal of the precaps and recaps which bridge the commercial break. Extra contextual information is provided for an audience more unfamiliar with the grand narratives of American history, the music is stripped back in line with the British version and the measured tone of Mark Strong's voice-over is reinserted.[31] Whilst the first-person voice-over ensures the centrality of the subject in the US version, the extra footage of Sarah Jessica Parker's interactions with her brother and mother and her 'tour' of significant childhood sites in Cincinnati afford an additional level of familiarity with the celebrity as the focus of the documentary. Despite the changes, the reviewer in the British broadsheet paper *The Independent* complained that Parker's 'noisy incredulity' and 'wide-eyed excitement' was 'not entirely British' (Sutcliffe 2010). Aside from the male critic's general dislike of Parker, her performance of self clearly did not exhibit the desired level of restraint that, for example, marked Paxman's attempt to shield his tears from the camera.

After the revelations of her ancestor Esther's involvement in the witch trials, an accused witch who narrowly escapes the court of Oyer and Terminer, Parker takes a moment for reflection in the Salem memorial garden. The NBC version, accompanied by Parker's voice-over, clearly foregrounds *her* experience. From the shot of birds flying against a blue winter sky, a medium close-up pans across a line of gravestones, the unfocused figure of Parker moving across the top of the frame in the distance. Her voice-over questions:

Parker: Who knows what would have happened to our family had the witch hunt continued? This has been such a moving experience for me; I wanna pay my respects to those who were not as fortunate as Esther. I'm visiting their memorial in Salem before I return home.

The narration is layered over a sequence of images of Parker walking through the snow-covered graveyard, pausing to look at one of the stone memorial benches, and the close-up of the engraved inscription – *Ann Pudeator. Hanged. Sept 22nd 1692*. The studio voice-over then shifts to Parker's location interview and her declaration that the experience has 'changed everything about who I thought I was.' A solemn string arrangement accompanied by soft power chords and piano signposts the emotional tone of the scene, quickly shifting towards the end of the memorial sequence to a more upbeat arrangement that has been used at various points in the programme to propel the narrative and the journey forward. As the *Los Angeles Times* reviewer remarked, the viewer is not allowed time to contemplate before being 'whisked away to the next "oh my gosh" moment' (McNamara 2010). The music here bridges Parker's return to New York City, New Jersey, and her mother's own incredulity on hearing the story.

The BBC's version of the scene uses the same sequence of images and is the same duration but the changes in voice-over, narration and sound-track have a very different effect. From the shot of birds flying against a blue winter sky, a medium close-up pans across a line of gravestones, the unfocused figure of Parker moving across the top of the frame in the distance. Here, Mark Strong's melancholic voice reveals the death toll of the trials.

> Strong: Between July and September 1692 the Salem witch trials claimed the lives of twenty men and women.

A historical fact which is 'thrown away' in the brief introduction to the trials in the US version, significantly, is not revealed until this point in the BBC edition. The voice-over pauses as Parker walks towards the stone bench and stops, and the close-up of the inscription *Ann Pudeator. Hanged. Sept 22nd 1692* is contemplated in silence. The scene uses the same solemn string arrangement without the additional musical layers of guitar and piano and as the scene plays out the soundtrack fades out completely, leaving Parker to her own silent reflections: the repetitive piano refrain, familiar from the British series, then returns to accompany her journey home.

There is much to comment on in the transatlantic translation of the format, and the rhythm, pacing, narration and use of music and silence reveal much about the different televisual vernaculars of the NBC and the BBC versions. Here, again, it is the sense of movement that is of interest. The insistent forwards momentum of the NBC version, com-mented on by the *Los Angeles Times* reviewer, is countered in the BBC version by an insistence upon reflection – the pause in the narration, the use of silence offering the personality and by extension, the viewer, the space for contemplation; a space which is nonetheless managed and performed by the grammar of the scene. It is the management of this space that I would argue characterises the public service value of the format in the BBC's hands. This has much to do with the subtle connections it leaves the viewer to make by him or herself and is achieved through the use of the third-person narration which opens up the relationship between the investigator and his/her investigations. This relationship between the explorer and the explored is collapsed in the use of first-person narration which allows the viewer little respite from the mediation of the historical via the personal. The possibility of an empathetic connection to the community is closed down in this insistence on individual experience.

This brief investigation of different versions of the same format points towards the productive work that can be achieved through comparative analysis. It is in the comparison between NBC and BBC versions of the same episode that the public service aesthetic of the British *WDYTYA* is brought into focus, and it is the programme's context within recent discourses of public service broadcasting that I would like to conclude.

Remembering public service broadcasting

Returning home to the original British version of *WDYTYA*, whilst I have drawn examples from later episodes and from the various international incarnations, this chapter has focused predominantly on the first two series of the show as broadcast on BBC Two in 2004 and 2006. The work done across these series established the format and nurtured its continued success. These two series also coinciding with the period of the BBC's most recent charter renewal and licence fee negotiations, the celebrations of *WDYTYA* and the specific nature of its address must be viewed in relation to the renewed public service ethos of the BBC in this period.[32] It is within this climate that I wish to suggest that an additional layer of memory is at work in the *WDYTYA* 'campaign'. Whilst the programme used strategies of memory work to reaffirm personal and national identities, the BBC used *WDYTYA* to secure its own sense of identity and remind the viewer of its role as an effective and relevant public service broadcaster.

Narratives of transition and crisis have become increasingly prevalent during a time of dramatic technological change and uncertainty over the future of television. Increased commercialisation, competition and the fragmentation of the television audience has brought into question the efficacy of public service broadcasting as a form of 'social cement'. As Philip M. Taylor comments 'the idea that television, as a medium which enjoys near universal social penetration, can unite a nation is in decline. The likelihood of an affirmative answer to the question "did you see on TV last night?" ' has diminished in less than a generation' (2001, p. 174). However, a show like *WDYTYA* might be seen to reinvigorate those qualities that Taylor laments. A ratings success for the BBC, often with sensationalist appeal, the programme is also significant in its exploration of national history and identity. It attempts to re-imagine British identity through the investigations of personal history, memory and identity. It also employs the significant popular appeal of family history research itself as a form of 'social cement'. One might argue that, in its careful construction of a portrait of 'New Britain', *WDYTYA*, alongside projects such as *A Picture of Britain* (BBC, 2005) and *Coast* (BBC, 2005–), marked a renewed public service broadcasting ethos that focused on the construction of 'Britishness' and national identity; public service broadcasting as nation-building rather than nation-binding.[33]

The consumer and audience research report on the first series of *WDYTYA* outlined, via quantitative data on the 'success' of the website and related family history events, how the BBC had fulfilled its campaign objectives. According to the report, 7% of UK adults claimed to have started researching their family history for the first time in the two months after the transmission of the first series. 61% of bbc.co.uk/familyhistory users said that they were new users to family history on the Web, whilst there was an 18% increase in first-time visitors to the National Archive website (in the last quarter of 2004 versus the last quarter of 2003). *WDYTYA*, as the forerunner of the genealogy show, may certainly have 'come to symbolise the kind of programme the newly public service focused BBC should be doing: serious-minded, but also accessible and popular' (Brown 2004); at least this is the assessment within BBC discourses. I want to conclude by suggesting how *WDYTYA* is tied to a complementary form of television memory, one which we might refer to as BBC nostalgia and is explored in more detail in the next chapter. It is perhaps not surprising that the programme was promoted as a jewel in the BBC crown throughout the period of the recent licence fee negotiations. Along with ratings success, the interactive platforms attached to the programme produce a form of public service that is tangible and quantifiable, in which the relevance of the BBC can be clearly visualised via statistics. *WDYTYA* is perhaps a key example of the BBC's attempts to secure and reaffirm its own identity through a period of transition and uncertainty. The show is arguably as much about our memories of, and nostalgia for, effective and relevant public service television as it is about family memory and national history.

4
Safe Returns: Nostalgia and Television

Derek Kompare's work on North American television examines what he refers to as the 'regime of repetition' – the constant recirculation of the nation's cultural and individual pasts in the present through the ubiquity of past television (2002, p. 19). His book *Rerun Nation* (2005) traces the historical development of the rerun on American television, from the industrialisation of culture in the nineteenth century to the emergence of the DVD market in the late 1990s. What clearly emerges in Kompare's work is the production of a constantly evolving and 'dynamic television heritage' (2002, p. 20) creating specific forms of public history and memory, both of television itself and the world it represents. Television is central to our understandings of the past and by paying attention to the recirculation of television's own past, the devices and forms of re-contextualisation, we can reveal specific attitudes towards television as a cultural form and attitudes towards our historical selves. As Kompare successfully demonstrates, 'how we – as viewers and scholars – "remember" the television of a particular time is inescapably bound to how television remembers itself' (2002, p. 31), and how television remembers itself is bound to the construction of broader social and cultural memory. Archive or 'old' television, particularly news and current affairs footage, forms the basis of much popular modern history on television. This chapter, however, has a more specific focus in its consideration of 'television about television'.[1] It is a focus which allows me to consider the complex interplay between the old and new, the past and present that we witness in television programming, as specific televisual structures of and relations to the past can tell us more about television's own memory cultures and their influence on the construction of broader cultural memories.

It is nostalgia that emerges here as the dominant framework through which television remembers and refers to itself. The term brings with it a long and contradictory history of critiques, uses and applications. Whilst I do not feel it is necessary to outline the history of nostalgia in full within this chapter, I will highlight a series of points and observations that have become central to my own understanding of the term and its relationship with television. The title of this chapter refers to the multiple uses of nostalgia within television cultures. Here, I use the notion of the safe return in several senses. It refers to the economic 'good sense' of forms of nostalgia television as cheap and populist programming and corresponds with the commercial safety of reproducing past successes and familiar forms. It responds to the conservative applications of nostalgia and the safety of the past in an idealised or anodyne form, but it also relates to a notion of nostalgia where recovery or return is not the object of desire but the relative safety of distance and longing.

Through two particular characteristics of the medium, television itself is seen as a privileged site of nostalgia. First, as I have explored in Chapter 1, both nostalgia *and* television are attached to the idea of the home and this is central to the resonances of nostalgia produced within the examples discussed in this chapter, from the different articulations of home in *Life on Mars* (BBC, 2006–7) to the period domestic settings of *TV on Trial* (BBC4, 2005). Secondly, and related to the home base of television, the medium's dynamics of closeness and distance can be seen to correspond with understandings of nostalgic desire. Susan Stewart writes that 'the nostalgic is enamoured of distance, not of the referent itself. Nostalgia cannot be sustained without loss' (1993, p. 145). As a form of longing that does not seek restoration, it is balanced in the play between past and present, sameness and difference, recognition and estrangement. This is a dynamic which similarly captures the iterative motions of television as an ebb and a flow, moving back and forth.

In exploring these ideas I will also take into account the ways in which nostalgia is nationally, historically and generationally specific. This becomes apparent in the construction of different 'Golden Ages' and the role of generational memory in remembering television. These are linked within a discussion of institutional nostalgia that considers television about television through an example of the self-promotional practices of the BBC.

Nostalgic frames (1)

Collections

Television is arguably responsible for the construction of a popular iconography of nostalgia, and though not alone, it can be seen to build and reinforce a series of visual repertoires which refer to a specific era or period, or combine selected and selective images, objects, sounds and soundtracks to connote an appropriate sense of 'pastness'. Here, the past is reordered into a collection – a list. The collection, according to Stewart, 'is a form of art as play, a form involving the reframing of objects within a world of attention and manipulation of context. Like other forms of art its function is not the restoration of context of origin but rather the creation of a new context' (2003, pp. 151–2). In this sense, what is central to the textual re-encounters with past television is not the recovery of the original broadcast or viewing experience but its positioning within new frames and contexts that hold the past at a distance and reframe it in relation to the present. Paying attention to these forms of re-contextualisation offers a way of approaching the significance of nostalgia television for understandings of television history and the cultural memories it collects and constructs.

Caddyshack (Harold Ramis, US, 1980), The Vapors' 'Turning Japanese', punk and preppy fashion, Strawberry Shortcake, Brooke Shields' Calvin Klein ads, designer jeans, Who Shot J.R.? This list makes up some of the 'defining' popular culture moments of 1980 according to VH1's *I Love . . .* series (2002–8). Based on the BBC series of 2000–1, each episode is dedicated to a year within the 1970s, 1980s or 1990s and hosted by a key personality or 'celebrity fan' of the period. The *I Love . . .* series, along with other list or clip shows, is structured by the use of clips with talking-heads commentary, offering a collection of moments from film, television and the archive coverage of popular culture events selected around a theme, a specific year or period and generally framed by the reminiscences of celebrity commentators.[2] As potentially the most prevalent form of nostalgia programming, on British television at least, list television invites the force of Jameson's famous critique of the 'nostalgia mode'.[3] Nostalgia, here, is understood to be conservative, regressive and subject to the 'market imperatives' of the culture industry' (Jameson 1991, p. 21). A critique of its manipulative and commercial functions is clearly apparent in the economic 'good sense' of re-presenting or repurposing archival material; the 'sleeping assets' of the television industry. The ahistoricism of such shows can be seen to further correlate with Stewart's observations on the collection: 'In the collection, time is not something to be restored to an origin; rather, all time is made simultaneous or synchronous within the collection's world' (1993, p. 151).

Forms of nostalgia programming such as clip shows and countdowns, and the programming of reruns on US nostalgia networks Nick at Nite and TV Land, have received limited academic interest beyond the work of O'Sullivan (1998), Spigel (2001), Moran (2002) and Kompare (2005). Yet, from the retrospective scheduling practices of BBC Four and its current trend for biopics of 'telly greats',[4] to the 'panicky self-cannibalism' (Brunsdon 2004, p. 115) of list television, the television archive is repurposed in a variety of ways. Examining the British television schedules across a four-month period in 2008 (August–November) the ubiquity of these forms of archive television became apparent. Though I don't wish to offer a strict typology, programmes fell into a series of categories: compilations or 'best ofs...' – *1001 Nights of the Late Show* (BBC4), *The Best of the Royal Variety* (ITV1); retrospectives, celebrations and anniversaries – *Dad's Army Night* (BBC2 – 40th anniversary), *Blackadder Exclusive: The Whole Rotten Saga* (UKTV GOLD – 25th anniversary); tributes and profiles – *The Unforgettable...* series (ITV1), *Mark Lawson Talks To...* series (BBC4); production histories, behind the scenes and genealogies – *Comedy Connections, Drama Connections* (BBC1), *Drama Trails* (ITV3); archive magazine shows – *Something for the Weekend, Sunday Past Times* (BBC2); revisitings – *Return To...* series (BBC2 – revisiting 1990s docusoaps), *I'm a Celebrity Get Me Out of Here! Biggins Goes Back* (ITV2); genre histories – *The Art of Arts TV* (BBC4), *Eric Bristow's Golden Arrows* (ITV4); representational histories – *Liverpool on the Box* (BBC4), *The Real Life on Mars* (BBC4); and television review shows – *Charlie Brooker's Screenwipe* (BBC4), *Harry Hill's TV Burp* (ITV1).[5]

With the move to multi-channel digital television services there is an increasing amount of television 'space' to fill. This brief taxonomy illuminates some of the ways in which the archive is reused in order to fill this space, and with the majority of programmes featuring on niche digital channels, which, according to Kompare, build their brands through the acquisition and promotion of programming appropriate to their image, television *as* history is at once both ubiquitous and marginalised.

Our interpretation of and the value afforded to past television in addition to the nature of the comparison that can be made between the old and the new, is inevitably weighted according to the presentation of television archive material and the strategy of re-contextualisation employed. The scheduling of archive television presents one form of re-contextualisation. Archival 'viewing strips', particularly common on digital channels, produce 'clusters of meaning' (Ellis 1982, p. 118). Framing original programmes through the commentary provided in behind-the-scenes vignettes or profiles of writers and actors, digital channels can offer bespoke viewing packages that compete with the 'added value' of the TVDVD extra. More widely commented upon as another form of re-contextualisation is the 'comic-archaic' quality of past television and how this is exploited through the 'camp', 'kitsch' and 'retro' repackaging of the television archive on the nostalgia network or in the list show; formats which emphasise these qualities through, to quote Tim O'Sullivan, the 'juxtaposition of the "dated" old within the flow of the new' (1998, p. 203). For example, part nostalgia show and part 'comedy of obsolescence' (Marc 1984, p. 8), Channel 4's series *TV Heaven, Telly Hell* (2006–7) captures an ambivalence central to forms of nostalgia programming. Borrowing heavily from the *Room 101* (BBC, 1994–) format, comedian Sean Lock invites a celebrity guest to share what they *love* and what they *hate* about television. The presentation of the selected archive material in this series is framed by the comedic commentary and observations of Lock and his guest, seated on either side of the screen, and by the 'highly-stylized' and 'retro-feel'[6] of the studio set; complete with disco ball, shagpile rug and the repetitive use, across the set design and graphics, of the iconic 'bulging-rectangle' of the old television screen (see Figure 4.1). Nostalgia in this instance operates as a particular mode, a recognisable style or framework through which we glimpse past television.

Figure 4.1   Sean Lock and Johnny Vaughan in series 1, episode 3, *TV Heaven, Telly Hell* (dir. Lissa Evans, prod. Objective Productions for Channel 4, 2006).

As perhaps the most clearly defined type of nostalgia programme, the 'countdown' often runs across several hours and is occasionally drawn from viewers' polls in listing magazines such as the *Radio Times*. Programmes such as *The 100 Greatest Kids' TV Shows* (Channel 4, 2001) or *Greatest TV Comedy Moments* (Five, 2005) present popular canons of television that are based upon the notion of the 'memorable moment' – but are also, through the process of canonisation, involved in constructing certain moments as memorable. Hierarchies of value also exist in terms of the shows, genres and forms that become canonised with a distinct privileging, for example, of drama and comedy. List shows can be seen to reproduce limited access to a canon of texts which in turn may be seen to reproduce collective memories of television, raising concerns around both the representation of television history and the management of those memories. For example, often voted as the 'greatest moment' in British television comedy history, Del Boy (David Jason) falling through the bar in *Only Fools and Horses* (BBC1, 1981–2003) has been cultivated through its canonisation and repetition as one of the great moments of British television. One must question whether the repurposing of the television archive through these nostalgic forms means we are simply being marketed the same commercially viable memories, reproducing a narrow view of both television's own and wider social and cultural history. For example, with regard to popular representations of the 1970s, Dave Haslam writes of the 'Abba-fication of history' – that nostalgia television produces an 'image of the decade dominated by a selection of the most anodyne, obvious symbols: the Bee Gees, flares, platform shoes and Abba [...] history without the rawness and unpredictability' (2007, p. 1). Televisual forms are once again involved in the process of 'taming' more difficult histories and memories, couching the past in the safety of the anodyne.

Television as history is subject to as many of the codes, conventions and trends that appear in history on television, where, to re-employ Kerwin Klein's line of argument, memory can operate as a way of softening and making history more accessible. From the C-list celebrities' reminiscences of *spangles* and *clackers*, to the staged encounter between the television personality and their archival past, memory and nostalgia are the principal modes through which highly selective glimpses of the television archive are viewed. Personal anecdote and reminiscence contextualise and lend significance to what can feel like the haphazard nature of the television archive.

For Joe Moran, nostalgia programming illuminates 'how easily the banal objects of everyday life [...] can be invested with affective meaning' (2002, p. 159). Both Moran and O'Sullivan position those texts that might be considered to be depthless and superficial in relation to the affective meaning they induce and the '*deep* forms of cultural and emotional (in)security' they invoke (O'Sullivan 1998, p. 203). What interests me here and what I will return to is how our response to and understandings of television's own history are mediated by forms, like the collection of nostalgic re-contextualisation. What is revealed are the ways in which attitudes towards television's past are constructed through a collage of past and present and categorised in various ways by autobiographical, generational and cultural memories.

Recollections

For me, 'television about television' has an additional significance in that part of the pleasures of this 'genre' questions not only what we remember but also how we remember. Nostalgia television is characterised by the playful address with the expectations of remembering. Here, a desire to remember may translate into the pleasure of recognition and deep forms of affection generated by nostalgia, yet this is tempered by the risk of non-recognition or the disappointments of mis-remembering. Despite these variable 'payoffs' the pleasures of nostalgia television are driven by curiosity and anticipation: will it be how I remembered? Is this how we once were? These pleasures in part reveal the successful 'hook' of the popular countdown format.

As a form of engagement, nostalgia is more about a desire to remember not to re-experience; to recall not to recover. My own understanding of nostalgia television is borne from Jean Pickering's notion of nostalgia as a 'leisure activity'. For Pickering, nostalgia 'seems to have something in common with Wordsworth's idea of poetry as "recollection in tranquillity", needing both distraction from immediate concerns and deliberate recollection for its manifestation' (1997, p. 207). Nostalgia television, at least in the forms I discuss in this chapter, involves the conscious and deliberate recollection of past television – television about television which re-works, jumbles and reframes itself, constructing and interrogating the relationship between past and present and our expectations of memory and recollection. In this sense it is related to Dyer's understanding of pastiche, which can illuminate 'the feeling of the dialectic of sameness and difference vis a vis the past' and 'sets in *play* our relationship to [that] past' (my emphasis 2006, p. 177), and similar to his model of pastiche it invites the co-existence of critical thinking and emotional engagement. As Pam Cook argues, in relation to the nostalgia film, the audience's interaction with the representations of the past demands a cognitive response, as well as an imaginative and performative one (2005, p. 4).

Cook's account, which seeks to avoid a traditional hierarchy and sees nostalgia as existing on a continuum with history and memory, forms part of a body of revisionist work on the term and a growing interdisciplinary interest in nostalgia and its uses (see Wheeler 1994, Tannock 1995, Boym 2001, Grainge 2002, Pickering and Keightley 2006). This is work which seeks to rescue nostalgia and its potential from more pejorative, conservative and simplistic applications of the term, and to complicate the notion of nostalgia as being essentially inauthentic, ahistorical, sentimentalising, regressive and exploitative (particularly in commercial terms). Whilst the evocative etymology of the word and its original use as a diagnostic label for the homesickness experienced by Swiss soldiers provide us with a relatively secure point of origin, the shifting meaning and variable uses of nostalgia since its conception in the 1700s have made it a slippery and complex concept which, as Adam Muller observes, 'even the most sophisticated of its critics acknowledge is paradoxical' (2006, p. 739).

Given its shifting meaning over time, particularly the perceived shift from the description of an affective response, to spatial displacement, to a sense of loss generated by a temporal dislocation, nostalgia, as Pickering and Keightley put it, is 'not all of a piece' (2006, p. 929). Here, I wish to employ the television drama series *Life on Mars* as a way of approaching and illustrating the paradoxical and playful nature of nostalgia on television, and to discuss how, in its play with space and time, nostalgia can operate as a mode of critique prompting reflection on patterns of change and continuity. It is in this comparative function that nostalgia plays a role in the negotiation of identities, communities and forms of historical connectivity; of how we were then, who we are now and where we want to be. Nostalgia can offer an escape from the present and an idealisation of the past, but it can also be invoked to reaffirm a belief in the progress of the present, and whilst nostalgia is always about loss, recovery is not the objective and the return home is not always welcome.

Life on Mars (BBC, 2006–7)

My name is Sam Tyler. I had an accident and I woke up in 1973. Am I mad, in a coma, or back in time? Whatever's happened it's like I've landed on a different planet, now maybe if I can work out the reason I can get home.

Life on Mars, which ran for two series, was a critical and commercial success for the BBC. A successful spin-off series *Ashes to Ashes* (BBC, 2008–10) set in 1981 followed and a high-profile, though less successful, American version was made for ABC in 2008.

After being hit by a car, twenty-first century detective Sam Tyler (John Simm) wakes up in 1973. The central enigma of the show, which became its tag line, is whether Sam is back in time, in a coma or simply mad. Trapped in the past Sam is teamed up with DCI Gene Hunt (Philip Glenister) and begins working in a 1970s police department. The generic playfulness and self-reflexivity of the series attracted much academic interest as the show itself became a framework for both historical accounts of the television police genre and an exercise in the evolution of generic forms (see Downey 2007, Chapman 2009). Nostalgia became the other framework through which to investigate the significance and influence of the series (see Tincknell 2010). In this account I will attempt to bring these two lines of inquiry together.

The shock of the old

The series draws attention to the processes of remembrance through a structure of both recognition and defamiliarisation or estrangement. In a sequence from the first episode, Sam is still clearly in shock after waking up in 1973 and is convinced his mind is playing tricks on him. Following one of many violent encounters with Hunt, we cut to Sam as he strides round a corner onto a busy Manchester street. When Annie (Liz White), a WPC and future romantic interest, catches up with him he explains his motivations. Determined to shake himself out of it he states – 'my mind can only invent so much detail y' know. So I'm gonna walk until I can't think up anymore faces or streets. I mean this is just...'. Throwing his hands out in exasperation, Sam's gesture motivates both Annie and the camera to shift their attention to the street environment. The camera then pans 360 degrees to reveal the world which Sam is now in. The stuff of 1970s everyday life confronts the viewer: shop fronts, fashion, buses, cars and so on become the content of this nostalgic spectacle. As the camera returns to Sam and the confused Annie, she asks 'just what?' to which he replies with increasing bafflement – 'it's just madness!'

John Caughie has written that 'our glimpses of old television [...] seem to function – like old photographs – as a kind of *musée imaginaire*, a museum which, as Andreas Huyssen suggests, may remind us of the non-synchronicity of the past, of our difference from ourselves' (2000,

p. 13). What we might refer to as the 'shock of the old' refers back to television's 'comedy of obsolescence' and the 'comic-archaic' quality of past television. However, this 'shock' presents itself in a different way in this series, allowing us to examine 'our difference from ourselves' as a nation. This is clearly expressed through Sam Tyler's reaction to the 'madness' of 1973, and the camera movement in this sequence signals Sam as our main point of identification as the 'shock of the old' is mediated through his experience. His forward movement pushes the camera back, locating his action as the focal point of the scene, and it is his exasperated gesture, as he throws out his hands to signal to Annie the 'absurdity' of 1973, that motivates the 360-degree pan.[7] One might argue that in *Life on Mars*, the past is not just a foreign country, it is a different planet.[8] The spectacular presentation of this sequence and the use of The Who's 'Baba O'Riley' on the soundtrack, which builds from the opening of the scene with the first verse bursting in to accompany the pan, helps to defamiliarise the 1970s milieu. But in the authenticity of its recreation of period detail it reveals another pleasure of televisual nostalgia existing in its appeal to living memory.

John Simm's performance of this 'shock' is central to the effectiveness of the opening episode and beyond. The 'waking up' scene, which follows the accident, reveals much about the significance of performance, particularly as this analysis is enabled by a cross-comparison with the ABC version and with Jason O'Mara in the role of Tyler. The two versions are extremely similar in the construction and ordering of shots, with the use of 360-degree pans, though this time revolving around the character. The dialogue of the original is adjusted for an American audience (mobile phones become cell phones), and in both, the use of Bowie's 'Life on Mars' shifts between the diegetic (the iPod then the eight-track in the car stereo) and the non-diegetic, flooding the soundtrack at key points in the scene (waking up and the reveal of the changed cityscape). These techniques situate the character within a new landscape which is rendered strange, spectacular and familiar.

Simm employs a range of gestures to signify Tyler's disorientation. His performance in the series is necessarily understated in comparison with Philip Glenister's portrayal of Gene Hunt, the unreconstructed male, all bravado and machismo. In comparison the intensity of the experience captured by Simm is expressed through the character's interiority, his vulnerability and his swagger – he closes his eyes as if he can't believe it, he gulps, he squeezes the bridge of his nose, he sneers at the 1973 policeman. He captures an impressive range of emotions without losing sight of either the gravity or the comedy of the scene. We cannot fail but to compare the subtlety and range of this performance with Jason O'Mara's one-dimensional expression of shock – a permanently furrowed brow.

A 'reveal' is constructed at the close of each version of the scene, specifically identifying the action as occurring in a different time but the same place. Simm, as Tyler, scurries out of the building site he's woken up on and encounters a billboard advertising Manchester and its 'highway in the sky' (see Figure 4.2). The billboard depicts the highway Sam was previously underneath and as he hurries out of the bottom of the frame, a crane shot tracks back and up and the un-regenerated cityscape comes into view. The 'reveal' of the ABC version is arguably much more disruptive and establishes a different form of shock, which breaks the continuity of both the performance and the creation of place and time. Tyler, in this version, doesn't leave the scene; conversing with the 1973 policeman, he turns around to face the camera and looks up. The cut is to a low-angled computer-generated image from behind Tyler as he encounters the Twin Towers, gleaming in the midday sun, they loom down upon him as rain clouds ominously gather behind (see Figure 4.3). The self-conscious and simulated presence of the World Trade Center at the close of the scene is an effective, albeit highly manipulative reveal, but this form of restoration breaks with the construction of a 1973 New York. Whilst the towers would have been a part of the past cityscape, their spectacular presentation here is on a completely

Figure 4.2 Un-regeneration, Manchester in 1973, series 1, episode 1, *Life on Mars* (dir. Bharat Nalluri, prod. Kudos Film and Television/Red Planet Pictures for BBC, 2006).

Figure 4.3 Disruptive restoration, New York in 1973, 'Out Here in the Fields', episode 1, *Life on Mars* (dir. Gary Fleder, prod. Kudos Film and Television/20th Century Fox/ABC Studios, 2008).

different scale and refers not to that past but to a different one – their traumatic collapse on 11 September 2001.

The different reactions and reveals of the two versions illuminate not only the relative successes and failures of each, but also how the specific construction of both a period setting and the characterisation and performance of Tyler are central to the series' creation of recognition and defamiliarisation. It is from these that the tone of the relationship between past and present is initially created.

Over the rainbow

The makers of *Life on Mars* explicitly stated that the programme was designed to challenge nostalgic representations of the 1970s (see Downey 2007). Based on an understanding of nostalgia as a longing for an idealised past, *Life on Mars* certainly offers a more complicated world view – 1973 Manchester is far from idealised. However, it is Sam's central ambition to 'get home' that makes the series, first and foremost, a nostalgic narrative. The different articulations of home across the series layer the programme's play with nostalgia, both spatial and temporal. Home is Sam's prelapsarian childhood of 1973 Manchester (before the disappearance of his father – a mystery solved in the finale of the first series). It is also the future present of 2007 to which he is desperate to return, and it eventually becomes the present past of 1973 that the adult Sam grows to love.

The shifting meaning of home for Sam is clearly addressed in the final episode of the second series, when he finally returns to the future. A sting operation to thwart a railway heist goes disastrously wrong and, as the team are fired upon by an armed gang, Sam is lured into the safety of a railway tunnel by senior officer Frank Morgan (Ralph Brown) and promised that leaving the team behind and Hunt to take the blame Sam can now return home. The show's central puzzle is revealed as Sam, walking into the enveloping dark of the tunnel, awakens from a coma in a modern hospital to find Morgan, apparently his surgeon all along, smiling down on him. Sam's return 'home' however is short-lived. Unable to reintegrate into this future world, he is distracted by both guilt and a loss of feeling, and recalls the words of Winston, the quasi-mystical barman of the 1973 Railway Arms, to his mother – 'You know a barman . . . a barman once told me that you know when you're alive because you can feel, and you know when you're not because you don't feel anything.' The distinctive colour palettes of the two times are representative of Sam's attitude to his return home. The brown and caramel hues of the 1970s are no longer resonant of a tobacco-stained north rife with corruption and discrimination but of warmth, character and feeling compared to the concrete, glass and chrome-plated Manchester metropolis of 2007.[9] It is the present which now imprisons Sam as, accompanied by Israel Kamakawiwo'ole's melancholy version of 'Over the Rainbow', he pensively takes in the altered crowds and cityscape, continually framed behind blinds, steel handrails, banisters, chains and bollards (see Figures 4.4 and 4.5). Returning us to where the first episode ended, his liberation comes at the expense of his life as he finally makes the jump from the rooftop of the police headquarters, this time in order to return to 1973 and to rescue his friends.

The meaning of the shift is not ambiguous and what is of interest is, first, how it responds to a growing familiarity with the world of 1973 and the affection built for the series' characters. Sam's return to 2007 is very much a betrayal of the bonds built between the characters and with their audience. Secondly, Sam's reaction to the return home, the sense of deflation, disappointment and alienation corresponds with Boym's discussion of nostalgia via Jorge Luis Borges' observations on *The Odyssey*, where upon Ulysses' return home he becomes 'nostalgic for his nomadic self': 'Homecoming does not signify a recovery of identity; it does not end the journey in the virtual space of imagination. A modern nostalgic can be homesick and sick of home, at once' (Boym 2001, p. 50).

Figure 4.4 Sam leaves hospital, series 2, episode 8, *Life on Mars* (dir. S. J. Clarkson, prod. Kudos Film and Television for BBC, 2007).

Figure 4.5 Alone in a crowd, series 2, episode 8, *Life on Mars* (dir. S. J. Clarkson, prod. Kudos Film and Television for BBC, 2007).

The idea of home is a shifting site in *Life on Mars*, the recovery of which illuminates the distance necessary in retaining both nostalgic desire and the potential of nostalgic appraisal. We might consider this in relation to Boym's concept of 'reflective' nostalgia: 'the focus here is not on recovery of what is perceived to be an absolute truth (home) but on the mediation on history and passage of time' (2001, p. 49).[10] *Life on Mars* is both an example *of* but also reveals *how* television becomes significant for our sense of change and continuity. The comparative function of both television memory and nostalgia highlights the complexity of the relationship between past and present individual, cultural and national identities, becoming a 'rear view mirror' on who we were and how we have changed (O'Sullivan 1998, pp. 202–3). Here lies the critical potential of *Life on Mars* to invite 'complex viewing' (Nelson 2007, p. 179).

New wine in old bottles

In Sam Wollaston's review of the first episode of *Life on Mars* in *The Guardian* he wrote – 'It's *The Bill* × *Doctor Who* = *The Sweeney*, if you're looking for a mathematical equation to sum it up' (Wollaston 2006). This pithy pitch of the programme's concept points towards the potentially formulaic nature of the series (no less formulaic than Wollaston's form of popular television criticism) but also highlights the generic playfulness on display in the series. In *Life on Mars*, the detail of everyday life in 1973 is filtered through television's past and its self-conscious use of the crime genre. This is achieved through the use of an iconography of 1970s crime fiction as embodied by *The Sweeney* (ITV, 1975–8): to borrow some of Charlotte Brunsdon's descriptions (2000, p. 196), the 'squealing tyres' of the Ford Cortina and the 'macho heritage' of John Thaw's DI Jack Regan channelled by Glenister's Gene Hunt as the aggressive no-nonsense detective. But the series can also be seen to respond to the questions that Brunsdon sees at the heart of the police series of the 1980s and 1990s. The questions 'who can police?' and 'who is accountable?' clearly resonate with *Life on Mars* as issues of policy, technique, management and discrimination are central to storylines. These concerns arise principally in the cultural conflict between Sam and Gene and their different styles of policing (beer-gut intuition vs *CSI* style stress on evidence). Whilst the comic-archaic qualities of the formula provide a source of humour, the nostalgic play with a genre which focuses on particular concerns demonstrates how a specific dialogue with another age can be opened up.

Transported back to a recognisable televisual landscape, Sam Tyler's predicament in *Life on Mars* offers a neat commentary on the role of television as a portal between past and present. The television apparatus became central to the show and its 'time travel' narrative. Sam's 'life line' to the present is often connected via television programming. It is his portal between the past and the present as loved ones and doctors appear in the context of 1970s-style programming interrupted to relay messages to the comatose Sam. In his dream state it is the girl from the BBC test card that, in a nod to the horror genre where defamiliarisation becomes the uncanny, comes out of the television set and appears in Sam's room to offer cryptic messages about his predicament. In the broadcast of the second series, each episode was preceded by an aesthetic shift in time. In each moment before the start of the episode, the broadcast flow of interstitial segments appeared to break up, with the 1970s test card and colour bars flickering onto the screen accompanied by the sound of a rewinding tape and static. Television appeared to be breaking down or rewinding to a different time. The 1970s ident for BBC One was then cut in and the announcer's voice, marked as distinctively from the past via the received pronunciation of its 'BBC' tones and tinny sound quality, introduced the programme. This framing of the new within the old was employed through the promotion of the second series and became key to its branding, with trailers for the series and features in the *Radio Times* employing the respective style of the BBC's 1970s branding (see Figure 4.6).

The broadcast context and promotion of *Life on Mars* reveal the nostalgic value of television's perceived ephemera, in particular, the channel ident. The iconic images and sounds of past idents have been re-employed in recent years, for example, as part of Channel 4's 25th anniversary celebrations in 2007 and BBC Two's eighties season in 2010.

Figure 4.6 Trailer for second series of *Life on Mars* (BBC, 2007).

The channel ident has the potential to become an evocative marker of television memory through its repetitious use by a channel across a specific period of time. The distinctive use of graphics, music and sound which work to distinguish the channel identity for the viewer on its reappearance arguably crystallises memory and summons a series of associations with the period. What is also significant about the use of the 1970s BBC ident in *Life on Mars* is how the BBC works to reclaim as part of its own heritage the populist idiom of Thames Television's *The Sweeney*.

The generic playfulness and self-reflexivity that are on display in *Life on Mars* provide a way in which we can consider nostalgia as a specific form of televisual engagement. Here I return to the notion of repetition with a difference that characterised the narrative 'moments of return' in serial drama. In the case of *Life on Mars* nostalgia television's repetition with a difference is tied to generic production and playfulness. John Caughie examines the phenomenon of generic playfulness in television drama in his essay 'Adorno's reproach', and through Linda Hutcheon's work, which also considers parody as characterised by repetition with difference, Caughie suggests how complicity and distance might be seen as both a 'characteristic form of engagement in generically mixed forms' and as defining 'television's capacity to be critical' (1991, p. 151). In the example of nostalgia television it is arguably the movement between *closeness* and distance that defines this critical capacity but also allows for an emotional engagement with affective memories. This is perhaps illuminated in the strategy of recognition and estrangement and the playfulness with the processes of remembrance that mark a programme such as *Life on Mars*. Whilst the nostalgic text is inhabited by forms of longing and loss, a capacity to be critical is also produced by the nostalgic appraisal of who we were and how we have changed.

Whilst this outlines a form of engagement characteristic of nostalgia television, we might also suggest how nostalgia operates as a meta-generic structure; television might be seen to produce nostalgia for itself in its 'regime of repetition', where the strategy of re-contextualisation marks difference. Nostalgia television, however, does not always signal innovation and difference and is perhaps rarely thought of in these terms, as there is often an over-reliance on winning formulas and past successes. A competitive television market highlights the tension between creativity and tradition, and here, nostalgia emerges as a formula that offers another form of safe return.

Institutional nostalgia

The BBC and the rebranding of Stephen Poliakoff

With the competition from new media technologies and new forms of consumption (DVD, online streaming, downloading, etc.), the television industry, though not alone, faces much uncertainty. Nostalgia for the 'good old days' or a more secure time often arises as a response to moments of change and crisis. This might begin to explain the trend for remakes, because returning to existing and previously successful formats offers a form of security and quite often will deliver a pre-existing audience. Recent years have seen the return of a variety of earlier television drama and comedy successes as remakes, re-imaginings, prequels, sequels and spin-offs populate the schedules. Alongside *Life on Mars* and its spin-off *Ashes to Ashes* have been the regeneration of *Doctor Who* (BBC, 1963–89; BBC, 2005–) and the re-imagining of *The Prisoner* (ITV, 1967; ITV/AMC, 2009). A new generation has seen a new version of *Robin Hood* (BBC, 2006–9) and a fresh generation commands and obeys alongside the old in *Upstairs Downstairs* (ITV, 1971–5); BBC, 2010). There have been one-off visits to old friends in *This Life +10* (BBC, 1996–7; BBC, 2007) and *To the Manor Born* (BBC, 1979–81; BBC, 2007), and new histories imagined for the *Only Fools and Horses* gang in *Rock and Chips* (BBC, 2010).[11] American television has also seen its fair share of remakes with the return of, among others, teen and post-teen dramas *Beverly Hills, 90210* (Fox, 1990–2000) revived as just *90210* (The CW, 2008–) and *Melrose Place* (Fox, 1992–9; The CW, 2009–10), and sci-fi series *Battlestar Galactica* (ABC, 1978–9; Sci-fi, 2004–9) and *V* (ABC, 1983–5; ABC, 2009–).

Whilst connecting the viewer to their memories of the original incarnations, the most successful of these present some form of reflection on the original and build upon potential resonances. These remakes, reinventions and regenerations offer a point of anchor but also market the present and the future on the performance of the past. It is with this in mind that I refer specifically to the practices of the BBC as a way of opening out a consideration of the institutional practices of memory through the notion of BBC nostalgia.

The BBC's promotion of itself through discourses of memory and tradition has been discussed in relation to other texts within this book – the promotion of the BBC's mobile news service in Chapter 1 and the discussion of the campaign attached to the success of *Who Do You Think You Are?* in Chapter 3. What I wish to question here is how issues of creativity, innovation and value are affected when *this is what we do* (the tag line for the 2006 charter renewal campaign) becomes *this is what we did*, and resurrection becomes regurgitation. Whilst the BBC is certainly not the only institution to operate a form of institutional nostalgia, for the purposes of this study it is a useful point of focus for the discussion of notions of creativity and tradition in relation to nostalgia. As Philip Schlesinger highlights, 'creativity (defined as innovative programme making) was seen as the BBC's core competence, in line with long-established tradition' (2010, p. 275). As an example I want to focus on the promotion of Stephen Poliakoff as a 'jewel in the crown' of the BBC over the last decade, and the implications of this for constructions of a television Golden Age.

Stephen Poliakoff began his career in the theatre and has worked in film, but it is for his television work, produced during his 30-year relationship with the BBC where he is often both writer and director of his work, that he is best known. Poliakoff's first major television success was the BAFTA award-winning *Caught on a Train* (BBC2, 1980) made for *BBC2 Playhouse* and starring Peggy Ashcroft and Michael Kitchen. However, that level of success wasn't revisited until 1999 when *Shooting the Past* was broadcast. *Shooting the Past* is seen to be the first part of what Poliakoff has described as an unconnected trilogy, followed by *Perfect Strangers* in 2001 and *The Lost Prince* in 2003. Whilst all three dramas were popular and critically acclaimed, *The Lost Prince* has been Poliakoff's biggest success to date, with ratings of 13 million and an Emmy award win. The success of this trilogy secured Poliakoff's status within a 'great tradition' of British television drama but also within the BBC. Following *The Lost Prince* he was commissioned to write and direct two television films for the broadcaster – *Friends and Crocodiles* (2005) and *Gideon's Daughter* (2006) – and his status as 'quality television auteur' was secured across two more high-profile productions, *Joe's Palace* and *Capturing Mary*, co-produced with the stable of American quality television drama, HBO, and broadcast in 2007.

A fascination with the archive, themes of memory, nostalgia and history, and concerns with modernity, technological and institutional change have been consistent points of interest across Poliakoff's work, along with a distinctive style which I have characterised elsewhere as 'slow television'. What I am interested in here is how Poliakoff himself is constructed as an object of nostalgia and how this feeds both into the legacy of the single play as the 'Golden Age' of British television and lines of tradition emphasised by the BBC's self-image. One might note how the nostalgic promotion of Poliakoff is exaggerated in comparison with other veteran British television dramatists such as Jimmy McGovern or Alan Bleasdale. Working within social realist traditions of television drama, the contemporary edge of their work arguably doesn't complement, to the same extent as Poliakoff's, the nostalgic rhetoric of the BBC.

Poliakoff, as a contemporary television dramatist, is seen to hold a distinct and singular position, licensed with an unusually high level of artistic freedom within the BBC. Though the stress on the unique and original quality of his work is drawn from a romantic notion of the creative artist, he is constructed in the reviews of his work as a rarity, even an oddity – a leftover from a 'Golden Age' of British television who brings with him the 'qualities' of that age, notably the perceived creative freedom subsequently lost during the Birt era at the BBC. This is evidenced through both reviewers' and Poliakoff's lamentations on the demise of the single play. It is with a nostalgic inflection that Poliakoff introduced his first choice of record on *Desert Island Discs* (18 March 2005); for Poliakoff, Dusty Springfield conjures up the image of the woman featured on the opening credits of *The Wednesday Play* (BBC, 1964–70), and reminds him of 'those exciting days when you never knew what you were going to see on television'. The invocation of a more exciting time or even a time when drama was more 'valued' seems to play upon the current climate in television and the nostalgia for its own history. Poliakoff's unique position in contemporary drama may be because of his evocation of a drama past – a sentiment that is supported by Robin Nelson, who sees Poliakoff as part of the 'British single play tradition'. As both writer and director 'Poliakoff's work is as close to "authored drama" as it is possible to be' (2006, p. 124).

An article from *The Guardian* by Mark Lawson on Poliakoff and *Perfect Strangers* is itself entitled 'Like Nothing Else', and in which he writes:

> After the award-winning *Shooting the Past* [...] comes *Perfect Strangers* (BBC2), which, once again, feels like nothing else in the schedules. Poliakoff is also given the rare accolade for a living writer of a tie-in documentary: *Stephen Poliakoff: Shooting the Present* (BBC2). This also marks a shift in television history. A Late Show-type project in the old Late Show slot, it stands, like the drama that inspired it, as a treat that would once have been taken for granted by the viewer.
>
> (Lawson 2001)

In Graham Murdock's early investigation into the promotion of authorship and creativity within broadcasting institutions, he argues that the

promotion of such elements 'lies at the heart of the broadcasters' presentation of themselves as guarantors of cultural diversity and patrons
of the contemporary arts, elements which are central to their claims to
responsibility and public service' (1980, p. 20). Murdock argues that this
is not simply a question of self-presentation but that the value placed
upon creativity and individual expression is evidenced through the level
of freedom experienced by distinguished dramatists and authors. Whilst
promoting the broadcast of *Friends and Crocodiles* and *Gideon's Daughter*
Poliakoff proudly chuckled on *BBC Breakfast* (tx: 13 January 2006) that
the BBC was 'moving the news' for the first of the two dramas. Though
arguably an outmoded scheduling decision, it clearly plays up to the
promotion of Poliakoff and his work as rare and valuable BBC commodi-
ties – 'must-see-event-drama' which was accompanied by a season of his
work on BBC Four and a second documentary on the dramatist entitled
Stephen Poliakoff: A Brief History of Now (BBC4, 2006).[12] It is in the opening of this documentary that Poliakoff is praised by a series of actors
and critics in a selection of sound bites that testify to his 'vision', 'creativity' and 'autonomy'. Poliakoff is presented as a master storyteller,
and among the montage of sound bites and extracts from his work
he is filmed walking across a windswept park. As he pauses to observe
his environment, the low angle of the camera positions Poliakoff, with
unkempt beard and crumpled suit, against the sky and backlit by the
evening sun, creating a marketable vision of the television auteur as
romantic artist.

The BBC's nostalgic promotion of Poliakoff as both one of a kind and
as part of the lost tradition of the single play and the creative freedom
associated with it might be read as a response to the current period
of technological and institutional uncertainty and transition, where
the renewed emphasis on its public service tradition forms part of a
response to competition and digitisation. It is possible to read *Shooting
the Past*, in particular, as a meditation on modernity and technological
change with a specifically self-reflexive content. Poliakoff's own unique
30-year relationship with the BBC has lent him a certain insight into the
changes within the institution, and parallels may be drawn between the
threat brought to the archive by Anderson and the '21st School' and the
increased bureaucratisation of the BBC. As revealed by another profile
of the dramatist in *The Guardian*:

> Poliakoff is well aware of the post-Birt climate in which he is now
> working: too much damage was done to creative drama by the suits
> with their 'Producer's Choice' – which translated as a mission to

downsize or tame the unreliable creatives. The BBC now has a bad conscience. 'In the past few years there had been a huge shrinkage in drama output,' Poliakoff says. 'There was a department that used to be called television plays. It completely vanished one summer, unmourned and largely unremarked by the media. It was the destruction of the single film or play. I was surprised they got away with it, but they did. John Birt should be forever ashamed.'

(Lennon 2001)

However, the obsessive 'going back over things' that Sarah Cardwell (2005, p. 191) identifies as a key feature of Poliakoff's form of storytelling also illuminates how a continued preoccupation with certain stylistic and thematic concerns might be seen to exhibit a form of authored art television which is not only slowed down, but which has also become stuck in a quagmire of memory and the nostalgia for former glories. In this example, we might see the production of nostalgia as an increasingly institutional practice that reflects the particular situation of a national television broadcaster. Nostalgia, in this case, functions as both a response to a loss of creative freedom, the desire to recapture what has been lost, and as a solution to a loss of creative freedom: the ability to market, via nostalgia, past television forms.

Golden ages and generations

The presence of the television programme-maker, critic and academic within specific generational audiences underpins the construction of the 'Golden Age', a notion which, alongside the subsequent fall, is 'a key trope of the nostalgia rhetoric' (Tannock 1995, p. 454). This is a rhetoric which recurs across academic and popular understandings of the television Golden Age and reveals much about the role of generational relationships to the medium and the historical and national specificities of television nostalgia. Within the US context William Boddy's study *Fifties Television* seeks to account for the aesthetic and industrial changes within North American television of the mid-1950s which were seen to implement a shift from a Golden Age of American television to its commercial fall into a 'vast wasteland' (1993, p. 2). The transfer from the New York-centred production of live drama to the rise of the Hollywood film series is seen as largely responsible for the fall, with the former characterised by the 'autonomous teleplay of the anthology series' and the 'prestige of the television playwright' (1993, p. 5). The American Golden Age of Boddy's study, with its commitment to aesthetic experimentation, programme balance and free expression, bears a familiarity with a British Golden Age of the single authored play. In both cases, commercial imperatives are held to blame for the demise of standards and issues of quality and value that are fundamental to Golden Age thinking – an age which is tied to the romantic conception of creative autonomy and individual expression embodied in the figure of the individual artist.

However, in the North American context there is arguably a shift in popular constructions of the Golden Age, from the more experimental prestige productions of the early 1950s to the 'good old days' of *Father Knows Best* (CBS/NBC, 1954–60) and *Leave It to Beaver* (ABC/CBS, 1957–63). Derek Kompare argues that this shift occurred in the 1970s as part of a wider cultural nostalgia for the 1950s, where 1950s situation comedy, for example, re-running in the 1970s, became emblematic of more stable and simpler times.

> The primary spark in the Golden Age myth in the seventies (as opposed to earlier) was not so much the programs' 'liveness' but rather their '*fifties*-ness'. In an increasingly nostalgic era, past television's visual and narrative styles were increasingly perceived as a quick audio-visual reference to 'how it was'. Accordingly, the Golden Age tag was broadened to incorporate series and genres other wise far removed from the live dramas with which it was originally associated. It eventually blurred enough to take in virtually any series first produced and aired in the 'fifties', a diffuse cultural category that, since the seventies, has stretched from the end of the 1940s to the early Kennedy Administration. The Golden Age began to refer to the time itself (i.e., American economic and cultural stability) rather than a particular mode of television production.
>
> (2005, p. 109)

The political functions of nostalgia, and in particular its conservative applications, have been charted by Daniel Marcus in his study *Happy Days and Wonder Years*. Here he examines the 'significance of the 1950s and 60s for contemporary political and social life in the United States' (2004, p. 2). Marcus interrogates the dichotomous view of the 1950s and 1960s in American political discourse and writes that 'in the nostalgia of the 1970s, the 1950s became defined as a time of innocence, security and a vibrant adolescent culture. Many of the accounts of the time, however, also defined it as inevitably yielding to a movement into adult experience and trauma, a movement associated in public discussion with the 1960s' (2004, p. 6). Whilst these accounts of the 1950s revival in 1970s America highlight the conservative uses of nostalgia, they also clearly reveal its historical specificity; how, why and when are forms of television nostalgia called upon?

The various studies of the 1950s revival contrasted with Boddy's study also mark a distinction between academic and popular cultural applications of nostalgia and where the employment of nostalgia by institution and practitioner can be added to this dynamic. The American political and cultural discourse that characterises the 1960s as a traumatic 'movement into adult experience' might be compared with the British experience of the decade as 'swinging'. Rather than being based on the stability and apparent innocence of the past, innovation, transgression and experimentation appear to be characteristics of the Golden Age of British Television, with industrial changes, again, cited as the cause of the fall.

In the introduction to his collection of interviews with key British television dramatists, Sean Day-Lewis writes that:

> It is self-evident that there is much less space than there was for scriptwriting originality. The elimination of commissioning producers, able to cultivate writing talent, does not signal a better future. Centralisation of power throughout British terrestrial television means all decisions are made by channel controllers lacking any drama background. They look for known market appeal, 'drama demographics' as pointed by 'focus' groups, not writers' visions.
>
> (1998, p. vii)

Day-Lewis' attempts to 'beat a drum for a tradition' that 'looks to be slipping away' (1998, p. vii) are echoed in many of the contributions to Bignell et al.'s anthology *British Television Drama: Past, Present and Future* (2000). The collection features a selection of industry professionals associated with the Golden Age of British television drama who offer their recollections of and comments on the industry as it was then and how it is now. Irene Shubik, John McGrath, Shaun Sutton, Alan Plater and Andrew Davies, whether directly applying the label of the Golden Age or not, all appear to mourn the passing of past, more autonomous, working practices in television, or more specifically BBC drama production, often focusing on the demise of the 'single-play' as the short-hand for quality television drama.

Discussions of the Golden Age often come with disclaimers but inevitably draw upon the programmes and practices 'worth remembering' (McGrath 2000, p. 49). Whilst James McGrath protests that 'it was nothing like a Golden Age in its extreme backwardness, culturally, socially and politically' (2000, p. 48), his brief account is inflected with nostalgia for an age when 'people could feel responsible, could feel a certain autonomy, could feel a certain self-respect' (2000, p. 53). Tony Garnett somewhat oppositionally claims that 'there never was a "Golden Age"' (2000, p. 18) yet his rhetoric is steeped in the imagery of the struggle ('I fought a bloody battle with the BBC', 'I will carry on the fight a while longer'), mythologising his role in the politically and socially conscious dramas of the period.

John Caughie has delineated the Golden Age of British television drama as the period between 1965 and 1975. Whilst Caughie warns against the nostalgic reflections of Golden Age thinking where 'an unrecoverable and idealised past is used as a stick with which to beat the all-too-material present' (2000, p. 57), he argues that 'the idea of a Golden Age may be meaningful: when it refers to that historical moment when one set of meanings and values is being replaced by another, when the traditions which stabilised a culture are beginning to be questioned and rewritten, and when creativity seems to transgress the boundaries of received good taste' (2000, p. 57). By placing television drama within a consideration of wider cultural, social and political movements, Caughie's aim is to situate the Golden Age in the 'real', rooting it firmly in the 'transformations and transitions of the culture' (2000, p. 87), rather than leave its explanation up to myth and coincidence. However, the nostalgic potential or problems implicit in the idea of the Golden Age are locked by Caughie in the realm of fantasy and desire, and the implications of this nostalgia upon contemporary television production are not explored. If those rewritten meanings and values of the post-1964 period remain as the standard for British television drama, what transgressive potential can it offer us now; instead of looking forward are we just continually harking back? However, this potentially regressive position is much more complicated and explicitly linked to the social and political ambitions of a specific generation. Rooted in transformation and transition, the construction of this particular Golden Age is based upon the rejection of an earlier generation. The elegiac accounts of these writers and critics capture a sense of lost potential, for what could have been, but in their nostalgia for the future they also re-imagine a different way, a different role for television.

In this context the Golden Age carries a specific currency and can be utilised in both regressive and progressive ways. With this in mind, the discussion of the term within all contexts should engage with the question of *who* constructs the period and content of any Golden

Age, and for whom does the age remain golden? Boddy, for example, offers a reconsideration of the critical consensus surrounding television's Golden Age through his focus on journalistic television criticism, and the work of Madeleine Macmurraugh-Kavanagh on *The Wednesday Play* (BBC1, 1964–70) raises the important question of who is excluded from the mythologies of the Golden Age. Whilst Caughie acknowledges the gendering of the British Golden Age in its emphasis on the 'scholarship boys',[13] what are the implications of a television nostalgia that is gendered? The construction of a mythology of television drama authorship that is associated with 'maleness' and the single play and where the single play is emblematic of quality, authority and seriousness necessarily excludes female-authored and female-addressed drama from the Golden Age. Macmurraugh-Kavanagh argues that this 'ideologically motivated socio-cultural myth' is the legacy of *The Wednesday Play* (1999, p. 423) and that it has 'conditioned the roles of both gendered authorship and gendered audience reception in television drama. Thirty years on, women writers and female audiences are still fighting the legacy of this history' (2000, p. 160).

TV on Trial (BBC4, 2005)

Evidently inspired by the popularity of countdown and 'best of' nostalgia formats, BBC Four's series *TV on Trial* sought to find the Golden Age of British television through '7 nights of programming from the past six decades of British television, culminating in a live debate and the announcement of the best-loved decade following a public vote'.[14] Each night was introduced by two prominent broadcasting figures – one a champion, the other a critic of that evening's featured decade. The two commentators were viewed within an age-appropriate period living room watching and discussing the selected programmes (three or four each evening). The programmes themselves were framed upon a blue digital background, emphasising their position within the 'flow' of *TV on Trial* or via split screens which displayed the reactions and responses of the commentators (see Figure 4.7).

Alan Plater has written that 'there was a "Golden Age" in the one great sense that we were all young once' (2000, p. 68). What is perceived as golden is specifically tied to the 'youth' of the commentator. In the case of *TV on Trial* the 'witness for the defence' (at least in the first three episodes) is clearly identified as being a young professional during that specific decade. The 'witness for the prosecution' on the other hand is identified as being either a very young child or not yet born.

Figure 4.7   Chris Dunkley and Mark Lawson review *Steptoe and Son* in episode 2 of *TV on Trial* (dir. Amanda Crayden, prod. BBC, 2005).

TV on Trial specifically reveals how producers of a television heritage are influenced by their own generational references and preferences, as, in this example, different generations of ageing media professionals and critics endeavour to seal their own youth within the confines of a Golden Age. In addition, the format encourages a series of comparisons to be made both between the decades and with the present. Framing the archive image on the digital blue screen exaggerates the variable 'quality' of the image and prompts the viewer to make comparative aesthetic judgements. The selection of specific content and commentator also prompts a comparative critique of the sociocultural values of television. For example, journalist Kathryn Flett (the only female critic featured in the programme) is chosen to reflect upon 1955 and the representation of gender roles in sitcom *Life with the Lyons* (BBC, 1955–60), and British-Asian critic Sarfraz Manzoor is selected to reflect upon 1975 and the incendiary content of the sitcom *Love Thy Neighbour* (ITV, 1972–6).

Lynn Spigel has written that the history of television cannot be isolated into periods 'once we recognise that audiences are potentially interpreting new shows within the context of the syndicated reruns that surround them on the daily schedule' (2001, p. 360). Whilst we should question the effect of the interplay of past and present televisual forms, genres and aesthetics on understandings of television history and memory, the co-existence of pre-digital and digital aesthetics operates as a patchwork of television history, generating both nostalgia for past forms and a celebration of present achievements. An understanding of generational shifts might also be employed to make sense of this increasingly complex patchwork. For example, Derek Kompare reveals how the US nostalgia network Nick at Nite has been central to creating a sense of an American Television heritage, a heritage that shifts alongside the changes in line-up on the network that in turn reflects the shifting generations tuning in. Launched in 1985, Nick at Nite was designed to attract the baby boomer parents of the daytime viewers of Nickelodeon, harking back 'to the boomers' nostalgic TV neverland of the late 1950s with colourful space age shapes, bouncy pre-program bumps and promos' (2005, p. 181). This line-up and iconography, however, has shifted alongside the changing audience, with the current Nick at Nite schedule consisting mainly of 1990s shows to attract the parents of the new millennial generation. As another example of such a patchwork, *TV on Trial* also highlights the currency of the notion of the Golden Age and the use of generation as a framing device in which to 'interrogate' past television, pointing towards the potency of television's relationship to notions of generation as a phenomenon that, I would argue, merits greater attention.[15]

Nostalgic frames (2)

To quote Charlotte Brunsdon, 'television once was new, but is now old-fashioned' (2008, p. 128). I want to conclude this chapter by thinking about the recurring visual motif of the cathode-ray television (CRT) set and its bulging rectangular frame, which litters the design and graphics of 'television about television'. Colourful bulging frames and banks of CRT receivers line the studio sets of programmes such as *That's What I Call Television* (ITV, 2007) and *You Have Been Watching* (Channel 4, 2009–10) (see Figures 4.8 and 4.9). Old-style receivers self-reflexively frame the commentary and sound bites featured in satire shows such as *TV Ruined Your Life* (BBC2, 2011) or in heavily self-memorialised television such as the final series of the UK's *Big Brother* (Channel 4, 2000–10). These self-conscious displays of obsolete media objects and iconography are reminiscent of the celebratory 'consciousness of the televisual apparatus' as part of an aesthetic agenda popularised in the 1980s (Caldwell 1995, p. 13).[16] Here, though, the apparatus as object and image has become kitsch.

Susan Stewart writes that the materiality of the kitsch object is 'split into contrasting voices: past and present, mass production and individual subject, oblivion and reification [...] Kitsch objects are not apprehended as the souvenir proper is apprehended, that is, on the level of the individual autobiography; rather, they are apprehended on the level of collective identity. They are souvenirs of an era and not of a self' (1993, p. 167). Television as a kitsch object is both. An object of mass production yet historically associated with the intimate space

Figure 4.8 Studio set of *You Have Been Watching* (dir. Richard Valentine, prod. Zeppotron for Channel 4, 2009).

Figure 4.9 Fern Britton presents *That's What I Call Television* (dir. Simon Staffurth, prod. Unique Television for ITV, 2007).

of the home – the object and its iconography draw upon collective identity *and* individual autobiography. Perhaps no longer a signifier of modernity it has become an icon of nostalgia for these symbolic associations.

Across this chapter nostalgic programming and iconography have been read partly as a response to changes taking place in television, generating nostalgia for real and imaginary losses. Within a British tradition of public service broadcasting and the address to a national audience, television's transition to a digital, multi-channel era of narrow casting has been seen to threaten the medium's provision of a public sphere, a shared experience and a communal space. As an anxiety it is not unique to either British broadcasting or to television and responds to fears regarding the dematerialisation of digital culture. These anxieties have invested the television receiver with the paradoxical value of nostalgia. On the one hand, writing on the arrival of new projection and LCD display systems, Margaret Morse suggested that 'our box of symbols and words is emptied out, spilling husks of speech and gestures out into the air. Inside has become outside. And outside has become inside, without a frame to call us home from dreamtime' (1990, p. 140). Yet the television frame can also be seen to act as a form of anchor for an increasingly amorphous televisual landscape, as Daniel Marcus observes: 'In a geographically mobile society marked by technological and social change, television's screen has been an icon of familiarity, a stable location through which discontinuous, fragmented, and variable representations of American experience have passed (2004, pp. 4–5). Here we see how television is at once both cosy and old-fashioned yet invested with culturally specific anxieties, and it is as a paradoxical symbol of both security and potential loss that it has become a deeply nostalgic technology.

5

Television's Afterlife: Memory, the Museum and Material Culture

The stuff of nightmares, reduced to an exhibit

The first series of the revived British science-fiction programme *Doctor Who* features an episode simply entitled 'Dalek'. Rose (Billie Piper) and the Doctor (Christopher Eccleston) encounter a last relic of the Dalek race, the persistent pepper-pot villains believed to have been destroyed in the 'Time War', when they are attracted to the underground lair of a billionaire collector of alien artefacts by an anonymous distress signal.[1] It is the opening pre-credit sequence of this episode which is of particular interest as the long-running series self-consciously refers to itself as an object of memory by placing itself in the museum. The opening setting of the episode is an exhibition of alien artefacts housed in large glass cases inside a cavernous hall (see Figure 5.1). Various artefacts from the world of *Doctor Who* are featured in the mise-en-scène of the museum: something old (a Cyberman's head, created in 1966), something new (a Slitheen's claw, 2005 series), something borrowed (a milometer from the Roswell spaceship) and something blue, with the TARDIS similarly placed as an exhibit through the composition of the frame.[2]

First broadcast in 1963 it is the longevity of *Doctor Who* which has led scholars to respond to the series as a 'receptacle' for multiple forms of history, memory and identity. For example, in its changing constructions of 'British-ness' and understandings of British social history and memory, the programme 'provides the cultural historian with a window on the culture that created and embraced it' (Cull 2001, p. 95), with a key attraction of the show being its ability to 'map the shifting cultural landscape' (Chapman 2006, p. 201). The programme might also be utilised to map a shifting television landscape as the new *Doctor Who*

Figure 5.1   The Doctor and Rose in the museum. 'Dalek', series 1, episode 6 of the new *Doctor Who* (dir. Joe Ahearne, prod. BBC Wales, 2005).

self-consciously employs the knowledge of its own status as an iconic television institution. For example, the contents of the exhibition in 'Dalek' place the new against the old, inviting comparison particularly on the level of production design and special effects and illuminating how the show is involved in creating as well as prompting television memories. These memories are inevitably tied to experiences of change and continuity, of growing up with *Doctor Who* and the feelings it might invoke. This emerges as a central theme of the Russell T. Davies era (2005–9), with both storylines and a particular characterisation of the Doctor (as played by Christopher Eccleston and David Tennant) preoccupied with the passing of time, ageing, loss, longing and belonging.[3] 'Dalek' and other episodes, such as the reunion with former companions Sarah Jane (Elizabeth Sladen) and K-9,[4] arguably address those who have grown up with the series and find themselves, as does Sarah Jane, much older on the Doctor's return, and as the Doctor himself poignantly remarks when he encounters the exhibited head of a Cyberman, 'I'm getting old'.[5]

'Dalek' is certainly not unique in its use of the museum as a site of drama. In 'The Space Museum', a story from the 1965 series starring William Hartnell as the Doctor, the empty shell of a Dalek stands on display, offering a hiding place for the Doctor from the 'curators' wishing to turn him into an exhibit himself (see Figure 5.2). In series 5 of the

Figure 5.2 William Hartnell hides inside the Dalek exhibit in 'The Space Museum', series 2, serial 15 (dir. Mervyn Pinfield, BBC, 1965).

new *Doctor Who* an ossified Dalek, revived by the light of a time capsule, cracks out of its stony shell in the 'National Museum' to terrorise an already preoccupied Doctor and his companions. There are many examples across the life of the programme of the use of, not only museums, but also archives, collections and libraries as enchanted and enchanting spaces, and *Doctor Who* is not alone in employing the museum as a space for the encounter with a series' history and its re-imagining. The re-imagined *Battlestar Galactica*, based on the 1970s series, employs a similar strategy. It is at the opening of a museum about the first Cylon War, where relics from the original series appear as exhibits on board the soon-to-be decommissioned Battlestar, that the Cylons attack again after 30 years and the series is rebooted.

Andreas Huyssen's thoughts on the museum offer a way of framing both these examples from science-fiction series and the discussion within this chapter on memory and television's material cultures. Writing in *Twilight Memories*, Huyssen observes that 'fundamentally dialectical, the museum serves both as burial chamber of the past – with all that entails in terms of decay, erosion, forgetting – and as *site of possible resurrections*, however mediated and contaminated, in the eyes of the beholder' (my emphasis 1995, p. 15). Within these 'resurrected' fictions it is the site of the museum that allows a direct engagement with the programmes *as* history but that also draws a parallel between the museum and television as *sites* of possible resurrection.

The material artefacts of these two series are themselves not unfamiliar to the museum. A travelling *Battlestar Galactica* exhibition opened at Seattle's Experience Music Project/Science Fiction Museum in October 2010. In the UK *Doctor Who* props, costumes and memorabilia have a long history of exhibition, from the 'Doctor Who Exhibition' on Blackpool's Golden Mile (1974–85), to the touring exhibition 'The Doctor Who Experience' held in civic museums across the UK and featuring items from the new series.[6] A life-size Dalek also graces the exhibition space of TV Heaven at the UK's National Media Museum – 'the stuff of nightmares reduced to an exhibit', as the Doctor himself proclaims (see Figure 5.3).

For Huyssen, the museum is both the space of the archive and the exhibition, and it is the transfer of objects from one to the other, their re-contextualisation within the 'spectacular mise-en-scène' of the exhibition, which marks their resurrection. It is television *in* the museum which is the main concern of this chapter. In particular, I will focus on the curatorial practices of the UK's National Media Museum (NMM) and how they reveal some of the symbolic functions, meanings, memories and feelings generated by television's material cultures. Museum exhibition is where the 'past is made to speak' (Steedman 2001, p. 70); this chapter is about the stories that it tells and the afterlife it constructs.

Figure 5.3 A Dalek in TV Heaven (courtesy of the National Media Museum/Science and Society Picture Library).

The transformation of the archive

John Corner has written that the 'study of television has often been preoccupied with the contemporary moment, it has been the study of a perpetual present' (Corner 1999, p. 121). Whilst this remains true, more recent shifts in the status of the television archive have arguably prompted increased interest in television history and historiography (see, for example, Wheatley 2007). In *The Television Heritage*, Steve Bryant, head of the television collections at the British Film Institute (BFI), writes that when the BBC began its television service in 1936 no technology existed to record the live transmissions, and it wasn't until 1948 when the corporation opened a film department and started its own news film programme (*BBC Television Newsreel*) that the 'story of television archiving really begins' (1989, p. 5). For Bryant, the attitude that 'television was, by its nature, ephemeral and therefore not worth preserving' (1989, p. 2) along with various technological and operational influences meant that television programmes were not preserved and only fragments remain. Only with a 'realisation of the economic value of archives' from the mid-1970s onwards have the 'chances of television programmes being preserved' been improved (1989, p. 2). Bryant's early work on the 'story of television archiving' points towards the need to consider the increasing marketability of the television archive, but also addresses the fact that as television, as technological and cultural form, changes, so too do its forms of memorialisation.

Digitisation has increased the ease of access to and use of television archives, with digital dissemination projects underway at national, regional and university archives – examples of which, in the UK, include BFI projects Screenonline and inview, Scotland on Screen and the collaborative European venture Video Active. As educational resources these archives are offered in protected form and are only accessible through educational institutions. In comparison YouTube has emerged as a 'default' or 'accidental' archive, alongside the cumulative force of many online television nostalgia archives and forums and the phenomenon of the DVD boxset and its cultures of collection. Traditional models of television research and pedagogy are being challenged and the lines between academic and popular histories of television are increasingly blurred.[7] The status of moving image archives has prompted much academic interest, with special editions of journals and conferences dedicated to its discussion. Whilst a few years ago there was a fevered interest in the 'death' of television, its afterlife in the space of the archive is now at the centre of debate.

Lynn Spigel has warned, however, against the 'fantasy of total accumulation' (2005, p. 91) – a belief that digitisation will allow complete, unmediated access to the archive. There is a clear necessity to pay greater attention to the frames and logics of the television archive, in its digital and material forms, and increasing transparency in the work of archivists, their frames of reference and the selection policies (what is and isn't recorded, preserved, digitised) that they employ. Spigel's work offers a welcome overview of some of these concerns. Presenting an account of the history of the television archive in North America, she focuses on the logics of the archive and the reasons for preservation and collection (2005, 2010). Paying specific attention to the space of the museum and the exhibition of television history, I would argue, also offers a way of addressing some of these concerns and provides a framework through which we might analyse the 'curatorial practices' at work in such digital archive projects.

Spigel's work also raises questions regarding the role of the television archive and museum in relation to discourses of civic histories, architectures and tourism. Her account, in relation to my own research on Britain's NMM, serves to illuminate the national differences between these heritage projects. Most apparent is the distinction between the television archive and museum as private and public institutions. Here, the commercial and public service traditions of US and European television systems play a significant role in the creation of and access to different television heritages. Whilst this chapter does not stretch to include a comparative analysis of the histories and practices of international 'media museums' such as Canada's Toronto-based MZTV: Museum of Television, The Paley Center for Media in New York and Los Angeles, or the Netherlands' Institute of Sound and Vision, further research on these museums has the potential to illuminate national differences and similarities whilst engaging with the limitations, possibilities and practices of exhibiting media histories across a series of international examples.

In Britain, the National Archive, operated by the BFI, has functioned as the main institution responsible for the archiving of commercial television. The relatively recent formation of the television curatorial unit has provided a new focus for the BFI which, until then, had followed an archival procedure but the television collection wasn't curated or put into use. In 1988, the BFI developed the Museum of the Moving Image (MOMI); however, amid controversy and despite its success, the museum was closed in 1999. The site was regenerated as the BFI Southbank complex, which now includes the BFI Mediatheque.

Opened in March 2007, the Mediatheque is a free and open-access facility which allows access to a selection of films and television programmes from the National Archive.[8]

The museum in Britain responsible for the archiving and exhibition of television is to be found outside London. Located in the centre of Bradford, West Yorkshire, the NMM, formerly the National Museum of Photography, Film and Television (NMPFT), was founded in 1983. Along with the Science Museum in London and the National Railway Museum in York, the NMM forms part of the National Museums of Science and Industry. In 1999, a three-year and £16 million expansion programme was completed and the NMM currently attracts, according to the museum website, more than one million visitors a year. Sited near the university district, the museum, appearing like a curved wall of concrete and glass (see Figure 5.4), overlooks the Victorian architecture of the city centre, with a statue of a famous son of Bradford, J. B. Priestly, as its companion. As part of a larger complex it is situated next to the city library. It houses three cinema screens (one of which is an IMAX screen), three permanent galleries dedicated to film, television and photography, and a significant space for revolving exhibitions. Partnered with

Figure 5.4 The renovated museum, with glass atrium, was reopened in 1999. It was renamed as the National Media Museum in 2006 (courtesy of the National Media Museum/Science and Society Picture Library).

the BBC, the museum plays a significant role in the city's cultural life, hosting an International Film and an Animation Festival. The museum was central to Bradford's successful bid to become the first UNESCO City of Film.[9] In its collections the museum houses more than three million items, and boasts a larger collection of television technology than the Smithsonian Institute in Washington DC. Some of the objects that aren't on display in the galleries are accessible via the museum's research facilities and archive tour.

Huyssen explores how a contemporary fascination with memory might be viewed as a reaction to the 'spread of amnesia' and forms of 'planned obsolescence' in Western society (1995, p. 254). He goes on to suggest that the increasing popularity of the museum and the monument as central to this 'memory boom' may have something to do with the fact that both offer something 'that television denies: the material quality of the object' (1995, p. 255). Opening up a consideration of the relationship between television and the museum, he begins with a discussion of Jeudy and Baudrillard's evocation of the museum as 'just another simulation machine: the museum as mass medium is no longer distinguishable from television' (1995, pp. 30–31). However, his analysis stops at the notion of museum as television and doesn't extend to a consideration of television in the museum, or even television as museum. This chapter begins to interrogate the apparent incompatibility between television and the museum, and it is to the question of materiality that I respond as it seems to mark the 'paradox' or 'dialectic' of remembering and forgetting that Huyssen tackles. How can what Geoffrey Hartman calls the 'self-consuming present' (in Bal 1999, p. 180) of television operate in the halls of memory and history?

The romanticised image of the archive as dusty burial chamber sits at odds with the modern storage, preservation and security systems of the NMM archives. Whilst there is a strange presence of the old and archaic, in collections of early photography, for example, where the daguerreotype, tentatively uncovered by the gloved hand of the archivist, is both enchanting and terrifying in its ghostly singularity, there is a definite absence of dust which might have previously characterised the archive. But this absence of dust also exists in a metaphorical sense and is particularly striking in relation to the museum's television objects collection, viewed whilst on the archive tour; these objects are not really that old – they are just obsolete. It is difficult to get as excited by the shells of battered wood, black plastic and grey glass – they seemingly lack that historical aura that perhaps made the daguerreotype so moving – and in their number, Huyssen's observations are called to mind. Huyssen writes that 'our fascination with the new is always already muted, for we know that the new tends to include its own vanishing, the fore-knowledge of its obsolescence in its very moment of appearance' (1995, p. 26). The television collection at the NMM stands at a point beyond the vanishing – it is the grave/junkyard of television technology.

Carolyn Steedman writes in *Dust* that 'commentators have found remarkably little to say about record offices, libraries, repositories, and have been brought face to face with the *ordinariness*, the unremarkable nature of archives and the everyday disappointments that historians know they will find there. There is a surprise in some of these reactions, at encountering something far less portentous, difficult and meaning-ful than Derrida's archive would seem to promise' (2001, p. 9). The familiarity and everydayness of the television as domestic object seems to further counteract the possibility of being struck down by 'archive fever'.[10]

We might equate the fever-inducing dust of Steedman's account with Huyssen's observations on the auratic appeal of museum objects:

> The desire to preserve, to lend a historical aura to objects otherwise condemned to be thrown away, to become obsolete – all of this can indeed be read as a reaction to the accelerated speed of moderniza-tion, as an attempt to break out of the swirling empty space of the everyday present and to claim a sense of time and memory.
>
> (1995, p. 28)

How is this historical aura to be attached to the objects in this room, to continue the metaphor, how are they to be made dusty? For those unaware of the technological history written into the objects, and as with the space of the museum exhibitions, the 'sense of time and mem-ory' is achieved through narrative. By ordering the fragments, creating narrative meaning, the dream of the archive is fulfilled in its exhibition, where the past is made to speak (Steedman 2001, p. 70). An understand-ing of the context/use/history of the object, as narrated by the curator, for example, reinserts the object with a memory. Through contextu-alisation and narrative, the 'clapometer' featured on Hughie Green's *Opportunity Knocks* (ITV, 1956–77) becomes a point of nostalgia, as does the floor camera used on early episodes of *EastEnders* (BBC, 1985–), attached with the camera operator's prompt script authenticating its use. The early cabinet sets and homemade televisions become documents of social history, and the BBC clock that reputedly set the time for the whole institution becomes a source of awe.

Ordering the fragments

In Marion Leonard's research into and work on the exhibition of the material cultures of popular music histories she considers the conceptual underpinnings of popular music exhibitions and divides these approaches into three main categories: 'canonic representations, contextualisation as art and the presentation of popular music as represented as social or local history' (2007, p. 153). Whilst identifying the central approaches to the exhibition of television, I want to reflect upon the significance, difficulties and potentials of exhibiting television. Key to these reflections are the thoughts of the television curators at the NMM, drawn from a series of informal interviews conducted across the duration of this project, which also correspond with a series of changes at the museum itself and the television galleries in particular.[11]

The museum's original interactive television gallery was developed in 1986, to mark the 50th anniversary of public service broadcasting. After a £3 million renovation project, 'Experience TV', the new interactive gallery, opened on 21 July 2006.[12] One of the only galleries of its kind in Europe[13] it was designed to approach the 'story of TV' via technological, industrial, historical, commercial, cultural, political and personal/nostalgic exhibits and narratives (NMPFT press release, 2005). Part of the new gallery also houses 'TV Heaven'. Prior to the opening of the BFI's Mediatheque in spring 2007, TV Heaven was the only free, open-access television collection in the UK. Influenced by the viewing facilities at the MTVR in New York, TV Heaven opened at the NMPFT in 1993 with a collection of little over 100 titles from the last 50 years of British television. The collection now contains over 1000 programmes and is continually growing. The TV Heaven facilities were extended along with the regeneration of the museum's permanent television exhibitions and collections, and the facilities now include, after redevelopment, six small soundproof viewing booths for two to five people, a large viewing room providing seating for up to 36 people, and a revised system of electronic storage and exhibition.

The curators and project director identified for me the four key themes that they wanted to include in the galleries' renovation. First, following consultation with practitioners, they wanted to illuminate for visitors the work involved in the production of television. Secondly, they were keen to utilise the television objects held in the museum archives. Thirdly, they hoped to stress the sociocultural impact of television upon the nation and allow viewers to rethink the impact the medium has on their own lives. Lastly, they wanted to offer some understanding of the business of television. The four concerns of the project curators stress the desire to remember television 'through its industrial practices and social effects' *as well as* its 'creative and cultural practices'.[14]

Leonard suggests that the 'dynamic, experiential, transient' nature of popular music runs against the materiality of museum cultures (2007, p. 147). Here, the ability of the static space of the museum 'to capture or properly reflect the experience of listening to music and particlipating within its associated cultures' is questioned (2007, p. 148). These concerns are also significant in thinking about television in the museum and point to a wider anxiety with regard to the materialnot ity of museum practices and their apparent inability to capture the everydayness and ephemerality of popular cultural forms and practices. Discussions regarding the musealisation of electronic and digital media forms inevitably have a parallel with concerns regarding the use of these media in museum practices. As Ross Parry discusses, the physicality of tangible objects has for many centuries defined what a museum was. The development and implementation of computing technology and digitisation projects and strategies into the museum's functions and facilities prompted a great deal of anxiety. What emerged, according to Parry, was a familiar discourse of the 'real' (authenticity, uniqueness, trust) against that of the 'virtual' (inauthentic, untrustworthy, artificial), with two futures for the museum routinely presented. The first being a 'nightmarish scenario' in which the museum was 'reduced to a simulation' and where curators would witness the death of the object as the visitors inhabited only an online space. In the second, the museum became a 'sanctuary for material things in an increasingly digital world' (2007, p. 61). Whilst Parry goes on to consider the possibilities of utilising digital media in the work of the museum, paying attention to the exhibition of media histories might also serve to illuminate the potentials of these intangible forms in exhibition design.

However, the tangible object remains at the heart of the exhibitions at the NMM. At Experience TV, the emphasis upon television technology is clearly motivated by the remit of the NMM as part of the National Museums of Science and Industry. As the museum website outlines:

> The Television Collection represents the evolution of the techno-logical means of generating, storing and displaying moving images by electro-mechanical and electronic methods from the late 19th century until the present. It aims to record by associated material how the various processes of television production have developed, particularly in Britain.

This presentation of the 'evolution' of television as one of the museum's 'conceptual underpinnings' clearly builds a canonical and linear history of its technologies. Many of the items languishing in the museum's archives were put to use in the renovation of the television galleries. For example, the 'Race for TV' exhibit places the sets and artefacts from the museum's collections within a chronology which maps the changing styles and technologies of the television set, and recording and filming technologies (see Figure 5.5). Both the 'Race for TV' and the 'Future of TV' exhibits stress the science and technology behind the medium and its continuing evolution. Incorporated in the centre of this display is the 'Evolve Pod'. Sponsored by PACE, the digital television technology developer, it is designed as a flexible exhibit to focus on continuing developments and changes in technology, with recent exhibitions on digital and 3D television.

In a 2005 press release announcing the Experience TV renovation project Kathryn Blacker, the museum's cultural content director, commented that 'this won't just be an opportunity to enjoy some fantastic telly nostalgia – though there will be plenty on show. The gallery will also allow people to have a go in front of the camera and try behind the scenes tasks to really get under the skin of television.' A large interactive

Figure 5.5 Linear histories of television technology (courtesy of the National Media Museum/Science and Society Picture Library).

area explores the world of television production (from development through to post-production), where visitors can pretend to read the news or operate a television camera. This strong interactive focus was in part a renovation of the previous gallery's successful interactive exhibits, but also responded to the demands of the Labour government's 'Inspiring Learning for All' framework, which placed a stress on experiential learning and the development of skills.[15]

The success of the interactive elements of the gallery across its history clearly responds to a different form of materiality employed by the exhibitions, allowing visitors to get 'under the skin of television'.[16] The stress on experiential forms of learning marks the NMM, and the wider group of UK National Museums of Science and Industry, as a clear example of what Eilean Hooper-Greenhill has referred to as the 'post-museum'. As a site of mutuality rather than authority, 'the post-museum must play the role of partner, colleague, learner (itself), and service provider in order to remain viable as an institution' (2000, p. xi).

What emerges most clearly in relation to the gallery's 'production zone' and its open-access archive – 'TV Heaven' – is the role of both ritual and play within the museum and its intergenerational appeal. On one hand, the exhibits themselves offer a strong intergenerational stimulus; the 'Gallery of Televisions', for example, a display of television sets from across the medium's history, operates as a point of memory for older visitors, who remember living with the various sets, and a point of history for younger ones (see Figure 5.6). The museum itself and its relationship to different generations growing up within the city and the region is a point of memory and nostalgia. Keeping the same interactive features (reading the news, a blue screen 'play' area) operates as a way of both prompting and creating memories for the adults who came to the gallery as children and the children of those adults who routinely return. I am not arguing that this is unique to the NMM but that the life of a public museum and its relationship to local and regional communities is seeped in forms of memory that transcend and complement the value of the 'historical aura' of the objects on display.

Capturing the everyday

The material archive

In Glasgow, rather than residents having to travel to out-of-town recycling centres, the city council offers a collection service whereby large refuse items will be picked up from the street. On street corners and

Figure 5.6 The Gallery of Televisions (courtesy of the National Media Museum/Science and Society Picture Library).

pavements one often encounters the relics of our television lives – sofas, armchairs and old analogue receivers abandoned in the rain (see Figure 5.7). Citing Michael Thompson's work, *Rubbish Theory*, Joe Moran writes that 'while "something which has been discarded, but never threatens to intrude, does not worry us at all", rubbish in the wrong place produces unexpected meanings because it is "emphatically visible"' (2004, p. 65). It is the unfamiliar context of the familiar object that highlights the visibility of obsolete media technology 'erupting into the present with evidence of old habits and dead routines' (Moran 2004, p. 61). Contrary to the accidental and unexpected memories evoked by abandoned furniture and receivers, the museum is tasked with the conscious attempt to capture the everyday and the routine.

Though Experience TV is currently the most popular gallery at the NMM, the curators can be seen to face two particular challenges in exhibiting television. First, as a popular cultural form, the visitor comes with an already extensive knowledge of the medium in relation to both their own and wider social histories. The challenge of the curator is how to add additional value and interpret the objects for the 'expert' visitor,

Figure 5.7 A television set as an obsolete object (image: author's own).

and related to this is the project of 're-enchantment'. Discussing the 'museal glance of re-enchantment', Huyssen writes that:

> the point of exhibiting was quite frequently to forget the real, to lift the object out of its original everyday functional context, thereby enhancing its alterity, and to open it up to potential dialogue with other ages: the museum object as historical hieroglyph rather than simply a banal piece of information; its reading an act of memory, its very materiality grounding its aura of historical distance and transcendence in time.
>
> (1995, p. 33)

What does this 'glance of re-enchantment' mean for the exhibition of television? The Gallery of Televisions offers one particular example of this practice. Neither chronologically ordered nor extensively framed by contextual information, the display is striking in its breadth and height as visitors' necks crane back to see the top-shelf receivers.[17] Framed by a pool of light that sets shadows at play and emphasises the changing depth of the various receivers, the lighting design is also reminiscent of the blurred edges of the cathode-ray television set. An evocative and arresting display, we might see this design in relation to Stephen Greenblatt's description of the production of 'wonder' as a model for the exhibition of works of art.[18] By wonder he refers to 'the power of the displayed object to stop the viewer in his or her tracks, to convey an arresting sense of uniqueness, to evoke an exalted attention' (1990, p. 42). The use of 'boutique lighting' is key to this effect whereby 'a pool of light that has the surreal effect of seeming to emerge from within the object rather than to focus upon it from without – is an attempt to provoke or to heighten the experience of wonder' (1990, p. 49). Rather than emphasising uniqueness, in this instance the pool of light binds the objects together whilst illuminating their various dimensions – an effect which underlines the part/whole relations of the collection.

A dialogue between the objects is opened up in this particular display as they speak to one another about shifting designs and technological 'progress' in neither a linear nor a didactic fashion. By lifting the objects of television's material archive out of their everyday functional context and into the 'wondrous' mise-en-scène of the exhibition, re-enchantment is realised. The aim of the Experience TV project appears to be the provision of space, where visitors can both reinvest in television and reappraise its significance (as technology, industry, cultural and artistic form) in everyday life. Whilst the removal of the object's context is successful in this instance as a way of highlighting the visibility and significance of the material archive, it is the experiential histories of television that prove more difficult to capture.

Whilst experiential forms of learning have come to dominate museum pedagogy, capturing these experiential histories is a different and a difficult curatorial challenge. The ephemeral and transient practices of television as a popular cultural form find a material base in the routine and everydayness of the domestic home. It is this relationship that has been and could be used as an attempt to represent changing viewing experiences within the limitations and possibilities of museum exhibition. Putting the set back into its domestic context is a possibility that has already been explored by the museum. The museum's earlier television gallery, opened in 1986, can be seen in a programme entitled *Television Comes to Bradford* (BBC, 1986), broadcast to publicise the opening of the new gallery at what was then called the NMPFT. Revealing both the dramatic changes in the exhibitions and its points of continuity, the early gallery reconstructed historical 'scenes' from the development of television technology, its earlier forms of production and viewing practices through the use of mannequins. Television's 'family circle' of the late 1940s and early 1950s was recreated, complete with its generational and gender dynamics, by placing the receiver back into the context of a period domestic setting and scenario where a white,

TELEVISION COMES TO BRADFORD

Figure 5.8 Domestic viewing as an exhibit in the 1986 television gallery at the NMPFT, *Television Comes to Bradford* (dir. Simon Willis, BBC, 1986).

clearly affluent, family gathers around the set; father sits sternly in his armchair, the daughter crouches on the floor and the wife serves the drinks (see Figure 5.8). The now outmoded reconstruction serves as an attempt by the museum's earlier curators to capture an earlier form of viewing experience through its representation.

An experiential form of history that attempts to capture the history of experience is familiar from forms of history on television, which are often described as 'reality history'. *1900 House* (Channel 4, 1999) followed the lives of a contemporary family living in the recreated conditions of a family at the turn of the twentieth century. More recently, production company Wall to Wall revised this format in the three-part series *Electric Dreams* (BBC4, 2009), where a family, stripped of modern technologies, lived through the 1970s, 1980s and 1990s (a new year each day) and the changing effects and experiences of technology upon the home. In getting 'under the skin' of television, there is arguably the potential for museum visitors to engage in this form of experiential history. The conversion of period sets and the recreation of appropriate domestic interiors in which archive television could be viewed would allow visitors to try on, Iain Logie Baird, 'their ancestors' technological clothing'.

It is a notion that has possibilities for pedagogy within both the museum and the classroom. Writing in 1990, John Caughie observed that 'there is a real risk in the theorising and, particularly, in the teaching of television of opening up a gap between the television which is taught and theorised and the television which is experienced. Teaching seeks out the ordering regularities of theory. A television is constructed which is teachable, but may not be recognisable' (1990, p. 50). This is a dilemma exacerbated by the shift from analogue to digital. Though the current generation of students are old enough to remember the former, the ways in which to capture the experience of the analogue for a generation of 'digital natives' require greater exploration.[19]

The programme archive

The above suggestion illuminates the ways in which the material and immaterial parts of the television archive could combine within museum exhibition and beyond to illuminate television's various histories and ignite memories of the everyday. As Joe Moran has written 'the value of memories of the everyday is that they can shatter this illusion of timelessness, erupting into the present with evidence of old habits and dead routines' (2004, p. 61). The gallery's open-access programme collection 'TV Heaven' arguably presents a space where memories of the everyday can be invoked by the visitor, in this instance, rather than the museum.

Though on the same floor of the museum, TV Heaven is situated in a second part of the gallery. It is away from the interactive gallery and the displays of television technology and situated beyond a series of displays engaging with the 'social effects' of television. Through smaller text- and image-based exhibits these displays provide information on advertising, audiences and ratings as well as asking questions about the 'influence' and 'power' of television.[20] It is within this context that the gallery explicitly engages with visitors' memories of television through an installation of 'flashbulb' memory moments in British television history. Just before the entrance to TV Heaven, in a partitioned and darkened viewing room, there is another video installation featuring 'iconic moments of television'. Screened on loop in a small viewing space with a large screen, the installation provides a space for both learning and recollection, framed by the statement – 'You'll remember where you were and who you were with the first time you saw them.' The 'moments' feature the following events: the first man on the moon (1969), the fall of the Twin Towers (2001), the marriage of Prince Charles to Diana Spencer (1981), Live Aid (1985), the fall of the Berlin Wall (1989), Thatcher arriving at Downing Street (1979), the New Labour/Blair landslide (1997), England winning the World Cup (1966), the Challenger disaster (1986), Diana, Princess of Wales' funeral (1997), the Hillsborough tragedy (1989), the Coronation of Queen Elizabeth II (1953) and the Iranian Embassy siege (1980). Remarking that the 'difficult content' on display in this installation required great sensitivity, the curators chose a reverential treatment, creating a darkened space away from the other exhibits and abstaining from using voice-over narration. This creation of a privileged space within the gallery emphasises, not the tragedy or celebration of each event, but the power and resonance of television both to capture them and to reverberate down the years. This canonisation of memory is certainly not unique and returns us to the dominance of the news and media event in constructions of television memory.

TV Heaven is arguably an avenue for more open and less didactic forms of remembrance, yet, given this chapter's emphasis on television's material archive and its use within museum exhibition, what are the potentials and limitations of the programme archive? Is it possible for the contents of TV Heaven, as a collection of television programmes, to similarly re-enchant the visitor? If it is the 'very materiality' of the museum object that grounds 'its aura of historical distance and transcendence in time', then how does TV Heaven, without 'material' content, work as an exhibition space? How can a non-material form accumulate dust? Huyssen stresses the importance of the materiality of objects in the museum and their temporal aura as a 'guarantee against simulation, but – this is the contradiction – their very anamnestic effect can never entirely escape the orbit of simulation and is even enhanced by the simulation of the spectacular mise-en-scène' (1995, pp. 33–4). The exhibition of television in the museum has an interesting relationship to this contradiction of materiality and simulation as it is clearly situated in both realms. Television as object, technology and activity retains its material quality, yet the television image, according to Huyssen, is 'incompatible' with material reality (1995, p. 34). If we view television as a possible point of collective identification, rather than a 'vanishing act', then both TV Heaven and the wider gallery act as a place to share and affirm experiences and memories of our television autobiographies. If the museum and the archive are to be read as expressions of 'the growing need for spatial and temporal anchoring in a world of increasing flux in ever denser networks of compressed time and space' (Huyssen 2003, p. 27), then television in the museum might offer an alternative form of anchoring, allowing us to reclaim, via the television image, a 'sense of time and memory'.

On one occasion, whilst observing the users of TV Heaven, I was struck by the over-excitement of two middle-aged men from north-east England, one of whom had a dramatic response to the possibility of (re)watching an episode of *Jukebox Jury* (BBC, 1959–67), an episode that he remembered originally viewing as a young man. Sitting in the archive, I observed the users processes of selection and the viewing of their programmes. As many users come and view in groups, this process is often vocalised and their selections are often validated through stories of personal memories. I have also seen single users feel the need to discuss or reminisce with the museum staff as though the experience of reviewing programmes that are important to their respective personal memories and histories produces a surplus of feeling that has to be vocalised.

'Performing autobiography' is a phrase employed by Garoian in his discussion of the display of works of art to refer to the memoires and cultural histories brought to the museum by the visitor, which enables both a framework for interpretation and the performance of their subjectivities (2001, p. 241). A phrase which Leonard also applies to the exhibition of popular music (2010, p. 177), it refers to a mode of engagement which is clearly not specific to television, music or fine art, but in the context of this discussion it illuminates the significance of the visitor's encounter with the television image to personal and collective forms of resonance. As visitors share the experience of remembering television, vocalising their excitement and forging identifications among themselves and with the staff, what you can witness in TV Heaven is the active existence of television functioning as a powerful point of autobiographical and collective reference for remembered lives.

To days to come/all my love to long ago

Although it only opened five years ago, Experience TV, according to Baird, is already in need of updating, in relation to continuing developments in television technology and media convergence. Colin Philpott, head of the NMM, has said that, 'As technologies converge and the lines between genres become blurred we need to reflect this and be the window through which audiences can follow, understand and engage in those changes' (in Spicer 2006). According to Greg Dyke, these changes must also be memorialised: 'It's the speed of change that's happening now that's interesting and that's what we need to understand – what is the impact? And, of course, we need to keep some of that in our collections, because that's part of our heritage' (in Spicer 2006). The decision to change the name of the National Museum of Photography, Film and Television to the National Media Museum, and the decision to extend its remit to cover and collect new media forms, is indicative of these changes. With a new foyer, a temporary Games Lounge (drawing from the National Videogames Archive) unveiled in February 2010 and an internet gallery in development, complicated questions about how to best exhibit a new generation of media technologies and how to draw in a new generation of visitors are being handled by the museum's curatorial teams. It is arguably the experience of media convergence that presents a significant challenge to the museum, both in the rapid pace of change and the blurring of the distinctions between media forms.

The Museum of Television and Radio in the US took a different strategy to tackle the changing media environment. In June 2007, it was announced that the museum was changing its name to the Paley Center for Media. According to Elizabeth Jensen in the *New York Times* the intention behind the change in both name and remit was to make the museum 'more inviting and its holdings more accessible', to encourage a younger generation of visitors and expand the 'pool of possible benefactors' (Jensen 2007). Whilst the museum never focused its attention on the exhibition of television artefacts, the 'center' further 'downplayed' its archive of television and radio programmes and recast itself as a centre for discussion between the public and industry leaders. The collections policy also became more discriminating, with attention being focused on the digitisation of existing collections and new digital dissemination strategies.

There is a clear difficulty in writing about the constantly evolving practices of the NMM determined, as it is, not only by technological innovations but also financial constraints, and particularly at the time of writing, a phase of deep governmental cuts to public services. What is revealed by the NMM's current collecting policy, though, is its unique attempt to reflect technological change and update the media histories it curates and to make visible a longer history of the relationships between media forms and their impact on one another. For example, with regard to the television collections, the key themes of the collecting policy include the impact of television technology development on other media and the analogue to digital transition.[21] The NMM makes visible the constant evolution of media technologies, challenging accounts of the revolutionary powers of 'new media' which are often predicated on an illusory understanding of television as a static and stable object.

In capturing change and convergence, the NMM is also a monument to media obsolescence. On 6 July 2010 *The Guardian* reported the 'death of the analogue television set', with all major high street electronics retailers stopping selling analogue receivers 'nearly 85 years after

John Logie Baird held his first public display' (Conlan 2010).[22] It is the transition between analogue and digital that has run through the course of this book as both an anxiety and a catalyst, central to television's own paradoxical memory boom, and whilst the museum endeavours to capture and interpret this transition for current and future users, the viewer's changing relationship to television poses new and continuing challenges. This is not uniquely the challenge of the museum but poses wider problems and possibilities for future engagements with television and its relationship to memory and nostalgia. This book has stressed, for example, the role of 'growing up' with television as fundamental to this relationship, and it is the experience of having grown up with analogue television that has framed my own memories and observations within this project and has determined my response to new television technologies and formats. This line of argument inevitably prompts a series of questions which cannot yet be answered – what different experiences, memories of and attitudes towards television will be formed by growing up in the digital era, and what effect will this have on the forms of television that are made, remembered and researched? It is my hope that this book might pave a way for thinking about television memories forged in days to come.

James Bennett usefully describes television as 'a technological and cultural form that lies at the boundaries of old and new media' (2008, p. 163). Blurring distinctions between the two, television, once again, can be seen to inhabit, evoke, construct, complicate and play with the relationship between past and present. The title of this conclusion returns us to *Doctor Who* and is drawn from a brief encounter between two Doctors in a special short episode from 2007 produced for the BBC's annual charity telethon *Children in Need* (1980–). In 'Time Crash' the TARDIS short-circuits and the tenth Doctor, played by David Tennant, finds himself occupying the same time zone as the earlier fifth Doctor played by Peter Davison (1982–4). Our heroes bicker and bond as they work to fix the TARDIS and as the fifth Doctor fades from view he bids farewell: 'To days to come' Davison remarks, to which Tennant replies – 'all my love to long ago.' This is not a collapse of past and present but an affectionate evocation of television's significance to our understanding of and relationship to both. It is in this ebb and flow that autobiographical and collective forms of memory and nostalgia reveal themselves as both central to and generated by the workings of television.

Notes

Introduction

1. Television memory canons are inevitably weighted according to national contexts and are particularly significant for certain understandings of national identity. For example, the dominance of televisual narratives regarding both world wars and the popular evocation of England's 1966 World Cup win. For Paul Gilroy, the 'obsession' with these events embodied by the infamous chant within English football culture – 'two world wars and one world cup' – supplies a 'wealth of valuable insights into the morbid culture of a once-imperial nation that has not been able to accept its inevitable loss of prestige in a determinedly postcolonial world' (Gilroy 2004, p. 117).
2. A characteristic I also explore elsewhere, see Holdsworth 2010.
3. 'The Turin Bomb: Making and Unmaking the Memory of World War II', a research seminar presented at the University of Glasgow, 17th May 2010.
4. BBC Four launched in 2002 and is a BBC television channel available to digital television viewers in the UK. Viewed as a 'cultural' channel, BBC Four aims to 'offer an intelligent alternative to programmes on the mainstream TV channels' (http://www.bbc.co.uk/bbcfour/faq).

1 Half the World Away: Television, Space, Time and Memory

1. For example, the work of Andrew Hoskins, Steven D. Brown and Nuria Lorenzo-Dus (and their research team) on the Arts and Humanities Research Council-funded project: 'Conflicts of Memory: Mediating and Commemorating the 2005 London Bombings' offers a sustained and interdisciplinary investigation into the coverage of one particular traumatic news event and the forms of memory and remembrance that follow.
2. Arrest of ex-president Chun Doo-Hwan (1995); Hong Kong handover ceremony; Princess Diana's death and funeral; official approval of the International Monetary Fund; presidential inauguration; millennium celebrations; President Kim Dae-Jung visits North Korea; attack on the World Trade Center; FIFA World Cup held in Japan/Korea; Roh Moo-Hyun elected president (2003).
3. For further discussion of these points, see Holdsworth 2010.
4. This music is taken from the score of the television drama series *Deadwood* (HBO, 2004–6).
5. One of the most famous examples of the black mirror is a circular mirror formed of polished obsidian stone, on display in the British Museum, and used by Dr John Dee in divination. Maillet's account, through the history of the black mirror, focuses on the small black convex mirrors, known

as the 'Claude Glass', and used in the eighteenth century as an optical device.

6. Taken from Boym's short essay 'The Black Mirror, or Technoerrotics' which accompanies this collection of images. Available at http://www. svetlanaboym.com/mirrors.html (accessed 11 January 2011).

7. In another short essay, 'Nostalgic Technology: Notes for an Off-modern Manifesto', Boym describes her use of 'off-modern': 'The prefixes "avant" and "post" appear equally outdated or irrelevant in the current media age. The same goes for the illusions of "trans." But this doesn't mean that one should try desperately to be in. There is another option; not to be out, but off. As in off-stage, off-key, off-beat and occasionally, off-color. *One doesn't have to be "absolutely modern," as Rimbaud once dreamed, but off-modern.* A lateral move of the knight in game of chess. A detour into some unexplored potentialities of the modern project.' Available at http://www.svetlanaboym.com/manifesto.htm (accessed 11 January 2011).

8. Though the loss of reflection in these contemporary screens might appear to contradict this argument, in Maillet's account he describes other possible forms of the 'black mirror'. These include those used by magicians and formed out of 'circular mirrors of paper blackened by carbon pencil or charcoal, those made of pure black woollen cloth, or else of wood with a surface slightly charred by a candle flame'. Neither reflective nor bright it is 'the color black [which] suffices to capture the gaze and to fix it so that "things" will come forth' (2004, p. 59).

9. Recent Christmas specials 'The New Sofa' (2008) and 'The Golden Eggcup' (2009) saw the Royle's living room swapped for Denise and Dave's house and Christmas with Dave's parents, and a cramped and fractious holiday in a caravan in the 'pearl of Prestatyn'.

10. Karen Lury offers a more sustained analysis of this in *Interpreting Television* (2005, pp. 157–61).

11. The project was a close collaboration between the Film and Video Umbrella, Artists in the City in Reading (UK) and the Ikon Gallery in Birmingham (UK).

12. Paul Watson's 12-part fly-on-the-wall series was modelled on the observational documentary series *An American Family* (PBS, 1973). More recently Channel 4 in the UK has resurrected the format with 24-hour surveillance cameras installed in the subject's home (*The Family*, Channel 4, 2008–).

13. The three remaining categories of Bourdon's typology of television memories are about specific, discrete events. 'Media events and flashbulbs are related to memories of actual viewing and concern the specific genre of news or current affairs. The fourth category, close encounters, consists of memories of events not directly related to viewing, and concerns 'real life' interactions between viewers and television personalities' (2003, p. 13).

14. Whilst these memories are drawn from a British perspective, different climates and environments will work to produce other conditions of viewing and other patterns and flickers of memory.

15. This discussion is indebted to Karen Lury who shared with me similar experiences of these phenomena.

16. Series 1, episode 7 (tx: BBC2, 23 November 2004).

2 Haunting the Memory: Moments of Return in Television Drama

1. In order, we witness the deaths of series regulars Ruth Fisher (Frances Conroy), Keith Charles (Mathew St. Patrick), David Fisher (Michael C. Hall), Frederico 'Rico' Diaz (Freddy Rodriguez), Brenda Chenowith (Rachel Griffiths) and, finally, Claire Fisher.

2. Moment (n): from Latin *momentum* movement, movement of time, instant, moving power, consequence, importance (*Chambers Dictionary of Etymology*, 1988, p. 672).

3. For example, the 'previously on' sequence of the 100th episode of *Buffy the Vampire Slayer* (The WB/UPN, 1997–2003) was an accelerating montage of moments/images from all 100 episodes, whilst an increasingly worn out Buffy (Sarah Michelle Gellar) comments in the episode that the 6th apocalypse they are facing feels like the 100th. The 100th episode of *Angel* (The WB, 1999–2004) sees the return of Cordelia Chase (Charisma Carpenter) for one last mission. The death of the Wisteria Lane handyman (Beau Bridges) prompts a series of flashbacks and the return of Mary Alice Young (Brenda Strong) in the 100th episode of *Desperate Housewives* (ABC, 2004–).

4. *Perfect Strangers* DVD (BBC, 2004).

5. Proust's distinction between involuntary and voluntary memory is delineated in Benjamin's essay 'On Some Motifs in Baudelaire' (1939) in which he cites from Proust's *Swann's Way* – 'And so it is with our own past. It is a labour in vain to attempt to recapture it: all the efforts of our intellect must prove futile. The past is hidden somewhere outside the realm, beyond the reach of intellect, in some material object (in the sensation which that material object will give us) which we do not suspect. And as for that object, it depends on chance whether we come upon it or not before we ourselves must die' (in Benjamin 1999, p. 155).

6. Faye Woods has considered the particular uses of music that are specific to the television serial format, such as the inter-episode allusive use of 'Hallelujah' in *The O.C.* (Fox, 2003–7), *American Dreams'* (NBC, 2002–5) use of popular song to tie together multiple storylines, and the end-of-episode musical 'Coda' seen in *One Tree Hill* (The WB/The CW, 2003–) (2007, p. 325–6). See also Julie Brown's analysis of the use of music in *Ally McBeal* (Fox, 1997–2002) and the 'dramatic recapitulatory function' of the final montage (2001, p. 285).

7. Caughie writes that 'art television seems to imply a viewer conceived to be intelligent, and possibly critical, "reading" an author conceived to be intentional, and possibly creative' (2000, p. 140).

8. 'The Book of Abby', season 15, episode 3; and 'Shifting Equilibrium', season 15, episode 20.

9. Nurse Lydia Wright (Ellen Crawford) wakes both doctors.

10. Season 15, episode 19.

11. The episode is also dedicated to Sheldon Zabel, uncle of executive producer David Zabel.

12. A self-consciousness that is additionally created through the extra-textual publicity for the final series and the promotion of the 'return' of Anthony Edwards; the audience is led to anticipate the moment of this 'reveal'.

13. This is one particular form of reflection as the storylines of specific patients also often work to reflect upon 'issues' of medical care and policy.
14. Callie Torres (Sara Ramirez) in 'Time Has Come Today', season 3, episode 1.
15. Forms of 'speech-making' are certainly not unique to *Grey's Anatomy* and can be seen elsewhere in, for example, the political rhetoric of *The West Wing* (NBC, 1999–2006) or the infamous emotional and verbal dexterity of Julia Sugarbaker (Dixie Carter) in *Designing Women* (CBS, 1986–93).
16. 'Bring the Pain', season 2, episode 5.
17. This storyline involves the niece of the chief of surgery who is brought into hospital on the eve of her school prom. Missing this coming of age event the chief decides to reorganise and host the prom at Seattle Grace. It is perhaps a more explicit example of the merging of teen and hospital sub-genres.
18. 'Time Has Come Today', season 3, episode 1.
19. 'Didn't We Almost Have It All', season 3, episode 25.
20. For regular viewers Denny is closely associated with death as the posthumous Denny has previously returned to the series in a hallucination sequence during Meredith's near death experience in 'Some Kind of Miracle' (season 3, episode 17).
21. A term regular hospital drama viewers will probably be familiar with, colloquially asystole is known as 'flatline' meaning a state of no cardiac electrical activity.
22. A line he consistently repeats throughout his mid-season return, the resonance of which is re-read in his revelation/Izzie's realisation of her illness – he is not here to support but to collect.
23. There has been a wealth of scholarship published in recent years on HBO and/as quality American television, see, for example, Nelson (2007) and Leverette, Ott and Buckley (2008).
24. Shot by 'sentimental motherfucker' Slim Charles (Anwan Glover), there is no mourning of Cheese's passing – the rest of the collective are merely unhappy that they are left short of his monetary contribution.
25. A key characteristic of the soap opera where time, rather than action, becomes the basis for organising the narrative, creating a sense of life carrying on even when we're not watching.
26. 'Port in a Storm', season 2, episode 12; and '-30-', season 5, episode 10.
27. 'Bad Dreams', season 2, episode 11.
28. 'The Dickensian Aspect', season 5, episode 6.

3   *Who Do You Think You Are?* Memory and Identity in the Family History Documentary

1. Academic and documentary producer Paul Kerr has spoken about the influence of *WDYTYA* on the production of this documentary in his article 'The Genealogy of a British Television History Programme' (2009).
2. '...and crucially in the slimmed down BBC, made by an independent production company. Little wonder, then, that the director general Mark Thompson has been citing it in his recent speeches' (Brown 2004).
3. Hunt cites *1900 House* (Channel 4, 1999), another Wall to Wall production, as 'the pioneer programme in this "experiential history" genre [...] with

its easy invitation to empathy, reality history failed to invite more search-ing questions about the underlying structure of the past' (2005). In recent years Hunt has also attacked *WDYTYA*, arguing that 'television history is now more about a self-indulgent search for our identity than an attempt to explain the past and its modern meaning' (2007).

4. 'The Turin Bomb: Making and Unmaking the Memory of World War II', Research seminar presented at the University of Glasgow, 17 May 2010.

5. Peter Sherlock's work on the reforming of memory in early modern Europe is fascinating in its illumination of the historical specificities of the under-standings and uses of memory. Exploring memory in relation to the construction of renaissance and reformation identities, he considers how 'Petrach and his successors sought to recast memory, not as a practice about recalling the past, but as a way of projecting the self into the future'. This 'new emphasis on fame and the desire to find genealogical links to the past led to an increase in the production of family histories from the fifteenth century onwards' (2010, p. 36). Family history operated as a way of fos-tering allegiances and commemorating the lineages of celebrated families. Employed to lend credibility, families often rewrote their histories, engaging the mythmaking services of heralds and their ilk (2010, p. 37).

6. 'Narrative Strategies and Emotional Engagement: How Genre and Format Deliver Audiences in UK TV History Products' *Televising History: Memory, Nation, Identity* conference (held at University of Lincoln, 13–15 June 2007).

7. The *Daily Mirror* TV Guide remarked that 'This is famously the programme that made telly toughie Jeremy Paxman cry' (Anon. 2006, p. 19), whilst Ciar Bryne wrote in *The Independent* – 'It is a sight few people would have expected to see on television – Jeremy Paxman, that most ferocious of political interviewers, reduced to tears' (2005, p. 5).

8. *WDYTYA*, series 2, episode 1 (tx: BBC2, 11 January 2006).

9. As Alex Graham stated back in 2004: 'It's not a very complicated proposi-tion. It is about people you are interested in, and taking them, perhaps, on unpredictable emotional journeys' (in Brown 2004).

10. *WDYTYA*, series 1, episode 9 (tx: BBC2, 7 December 2004).

11. Tx: BBC2, 12 October 2004.

12. Forms of archival aesthetics and storytelling have been investigated in John Corner's (2006) analysis of *Wisconsin Death Trip* (dir. James Marsh, 2000) and Holdsworth (2006) and Hogg's (2010) work on *Shooting the Past* (1999).

13. Series 2, episode 2 (tx: BBC2, 18 January 2006).

14. A sentiment that runs across key writings on photography by Walter Benjamin (1999), Susan Sontag (1977) and Roland Barthes (1980).

15. Tx: BBC1, 12 August 2009.

16. *WDYTYA*, series 2, episode 3 (tx: BBC2, 25 January 2006).

17. *WDYTYA*, series 1, episode 6 (tx: BBC2, 16 November 2004).

18. Simon Schama's *A History of Britain* DVD liner notes.

19. *WDYTYA*, series 1, episode 7 (tx: BBC2, 23 November 2004).

20. *WDYTYA*, series 1, episode 4 (tx: BBC2, 2 November 2004).

21. *WDYTYA*, series 1, episode 5 (tx: BBC2, 9 November 2004).

22. *WDYTYA*, series 1, episode 8 (tx: BBC2, 30 November 2004).

23. Nicholas Crane uses William Camden's 1586 topographical survey of Britain as his guide. In other examples, the tourist handbook of George Bradshaw is

utilised by former MP Michael Portillo in *Great British Railway Journeys* (BBC, 2010–) and Harold Briercliffe's cycling tours are revisited by presenter Clare Balding in *Britain by Bike* (BBC, 2010).

24. Series 1, episode 2 (tx: BBC2, 19 October 2004).
25. The BBC campaign objectives for the first series of *WDYTYA* were stated as the following: 1) To enable and encourage 150,000 ABC1 50+ BBC2 audiences to start researching their own family history for the first time; 2) To bring new users to archives and genealogical websites; 3) To give people a meaningful sense of their personal connection with history (in Sumpner et al. 2005).
26. *WDYTYA*, series 7, episode 5 (tx: BBC1, 16 August 2010).
27. Alison Landsberg also points towards a similar concern in her account of the success of Alex Haley's *Roots* (ABC, 1977) in 1970s America. She writes that 'while it enabled many whites to see through black eyes for the first time, what emerged from the experience of *Roots* was not so much a critique of white oppression as an appreciation of the importance and power of geneal- ogy [...] Rather than forcing white Americans to take a look at their own attitudes toward race, rather than forcing them to own up to the crimes of slavery, the mass media stimulated instead a fascination with the project of genealogy' (2004, pp. 105–6).
28. Gilroy's conceptualisation of 'postcolonial melancholia' employs the Mitscherlichs' model of a German post-war melancholia developed in *The Inability to Mourn* (1975). Gilroy's work explores 'Britain's inability to mourn the loss of empire' (2004, p. 111), arguing that, 'rather than work through those feelings, that unsettling history was diminished, denied, and then, if possible, actively forgotten' (2004, p. 98). Gilroy himself calls for more 'complex and challenging narratives' (2004, p. 131).
29. This argument is supported by both Paul Kerr and Ross Wilson's work on the representations of slavery on British television. Paul Kerr has written of his frustrations as the producer of *The Last Slave* and the reduction of a story of the last slave ship with multiple points of view to the single documentary about one man's 'personal journey' in search of his slave ancestors (2009, p. 394). Whilst Ross Wilson has written an account of the selective amnesia of the BBC's abolition season, presenting a 'preferred version' of history, one which emphasised the work of the abolitionists and presented a stable mul- ticultural Britain untroubled by the past by focusing firmly on the trope of 'moving on' (2008, p. 393).
30. MacIntyre, A. (2010) 'Lisa Kudrow interview' (3 March). Available at: http:// www.monstersandcritics.com/smallscreen/features/article_1538079.php/ NBC-Who-Do-You-Think-You-Are-comes-March-5-Lisa-Kudrow-interview (accessed on 2 September 2010).
31. An actor renowned for playing dark and menacing characters, his voice, whilst measured and controlled, is neither theatrical nor comfy – it might be described instead as resonating with an uneasy melancholia.
32. After the perceived slippage of public service provision in a period of increased competition, commercial pressures and the battle for ratings, along with the shift towards 'Digital Britain', 2006 saw intense debates around the ten-year Royal charter review and the future of the BBC. It is within the context of this period that the BBC attempts to revalidate its role as a

public service provider and justify the continuation of, and argue for, an above-inflation increase in the licence fee.

33. A strategy which also becomes apparent in Niki Strange's account of the BBC's changes to commissioning and the development of the 'bundled project' in the same era. She writes that 'in tying in this content' [*Great Britons* (BBC, 2002), *The Big Read* (BBC, 2003), *A Picture of Britain* (BBC, 2005)] with a range of initiatives with schools, libraries, national literacy organisations, and charities, as well as with publishers and book retailers, the BBC sought to emphasise its successful role less as broadcaster than as orchestrator of a multi-partnered, multi-platform campaign whose public service was in generating debates around, and reflections on, national identity and, also, personal 'transformation' (2010, p. 139).

4 Safe Returns: Nostalgia and Television

1. I am not charting a history of television about television nor am I examining the operations of the market for archival material, its distribution and use – though these are both lines of research that would add greatly to our knowledge of public and commercial uses and understandings of television history.

2. In the US context the 'clip show' generally refers to an episode in a series that consists primarily of excerpts from previous episodes, generally depicted as a sequence of flashbacks given plausibility by a narrative frame. Despite being heavily parodied within popular American culture, they remain a popular device that allows audiences to 'catch-up' with narrative events and have been recently employed in *Lost* (ABC, 2004–10) and *Grey's Anatomy*.

3. Jameson's critique of the 'nostalgia mode' in his *Postmodernism* is a commonly cited example in discussions of nostalgia and nostalgia television. He argues that the 'past as "referent" finds itself gradually bracketed, and then effaced altogether, leaving us with nothing but texts' (1991, p. 18). Nostalgia, in Jameson's terms, is ahistorical, sentimentalising and represents the decline in 'our lived possibility of experiencing history in some active way' (1991, p. 21).

4. Recent years have seen a series of biopics and nostalgic retellings of the lives and careers of some of Britain's most popular television performers. For example, *Fantabulosa! The Kenneth Williams Story* (BBC4, 2006), *Fear of Fanny* (BBC4, 2006), *The Curse of Steptoe* (BBC4, 2008), *Eric and Ernie* (BBC2, 2010) and *Hattie* (BBC4, 2011).

5. These examples are representative of the categories, not a complete list of the programmes scheduled within that period.

6. Presenting a sustained investigation of nostalgia networks on US television, Derek Kompare refers to the ' "boutique" model of television repetition' which creates 'highly stylized spaces for showcasing past television programmes' (2005, p. xvii.).

7. Annie, on the other hand, is clearly a part of the 1973 world. She is already within the scene when Sam enters and is increasingly bemused by his erratic behaviour.

8. See the famous introduction to J. P. Hartley's *The Go-Between* (1953): 'The past is a foreign country; they do things differently there.'
9. A production style which will itself become dated.
10. The neat etymological dissection of the word (*nos* meaning 'home' and *algia* meaning 'pain') allows Svetlana Boym to conceptualise two variants of nostalgia; 'restorative' nostalgia stresses the first half of the term and 'proposes to rebuild the lost home and patch up the memory gaps', whilst 'reflective' nostalgia 'dwells in *algia*, in longing and loss, the imperfect process of remembrance' (2001, pp. 49–50).
11. There have also been a series of returning quiz and gameshow formats including *Family Fortunes* (ITV, 1980–2002) revived as *All Star Family Fortunes* (ITV, 2006–), *Gladiators* (ITV, 1992–2000; ITV, 2008), *Shooting Stars* (BBC2, 1993–7; BBC2, 2008–) and a compendium of Saturday teatime favourites in *Ant and Dec's Gameshow Marathon* (ITV, 2005–7).
12. The broadcasts were also preceded by a screening and interview with Poliakoff and his leading actors at the National Film Theatre in London.
13. The historical narrative goes that the process of rapid recruitment from a specific politically aware generation in the wake of the Pilkington Report was seen to have a transformative effect on the BBC and its drama production.
14. BBC Four repeated the format in 2007 with *Children's TV on Trial*.
15. Emma Sandon's essay on the Alexandra Palace Television Society oral history collection, recorded between 1936 and 1952, offers a fascinating account of an example of the generational use of nostalgia. Her work reveals how, as part of a collective identity constructed in line with a British war ethos, that for the members of the society there was 'a generational need to be seen to have "coped"' (2007, p. 108).
16. John Caldwell, for example, describes 'CNN's use of banks of monitors that evoked video installations' (1995, p. 13). Both then and now the self-consciousness of the television apparatus works to distinguish the 'televisuality' of the content.

5 Television's Afterlife: Memory, the Museum and Material Culture

1. The Daleks have also been consistently destroyed and resurrected across the history of the show. Their emergence in Russell T. Davies' *Doctor Who* had to be expected and the moment the Doctor and his worst enemy were reacquainted was heavily trailed before it aired. For a complete account of the Daleks' history on the programme, prior to Davies' reincarnation, see Newman (2005).
2. The National Museum of Wales, Cardiff, is the location for the museum scenes in this episode and others, including, 'Planet of the Dead' (special episode, 2009), 'Vincent and the Doctor' (series 5, episode 10) and 'The Big Bang' (series 5, episode 13).
3. Promising less focus on the show's history and new monsters and villains to look forward to, series writer Steven Moffat took over as 'showrunner' in 2010 with a new Doctor (Matt Smith) and companion, Amy Pond (Karen Gillen).

4. 'School Reunion' (series 2, episode 3).
5. Nostalgic retrieval became a successful formula for the show under Russell T. Davies' control. With a parade of characters and villains returning from the original series, the Cybermen, Davros, The Master and even Gallifrey, the Doctor's extinct home planet, and the Time Lords were resurrected in Davies' last episodes ('The End of Time', pts 1 and 2, special episodes, 2009).
6. A new version of the 'Doctor Who Experience' opened in London in February 2011, destined for a permanent home base in Cardiff from 2012.
7. Alan McKee (2010) offers a useful comparison between YouTube and Australia's National Film and Sound Archive as educational resources.
8. Like the rest of the UK's public services the BFI has had its funding cut by the current government. At a time of radical change brought about by both an archival policy review and the savage cuts to its functions and facilities, the current status of the BFI as a national television archive is uncertain.
9. Due to funding constraints the 'Bite the Mango' world cinema festival was abandoned in 2010 after 15 years.
10. Steedman is referring here to Derrida's conceptualisation of 'archive fever' and his meditation on the politics of desire associated with this particular sickness (see Derrida 1996).
11. I initially met with Sheena Vigors (former curator of TV Heaven) in 2006 then with Kathryn Blacker (content director) and Claire Thomas (curator of television) in 2007. Blacker and Thomas had been heavily involved in the renovation and redesign of the television galleries into Experience TV. I returned to the museum in 2010 to meet with the new head of television, Iain Logie Baird, to discuss the success, the limitations and the future of the new gallery.
12. After consultation with focus groups and an advisory group featuring industry professionals, academics and learning specialists, the design brief for Experience TV was finalised in November 2005. Work began in February 2006 and the gallery opened in July 2006.
13. Another example is The Netherlands Institute of Sound and Vision. The focus on interactivity and media production along with a strong nostalgic appeal marks the difference, as remarked upon by Kathryn Blacker of the NMM, between these European initiatives and the 'intellectual' and 'historical' pursuits of the MTVR (now the Paley Center for Media) in the US (interviewed 17 April 2007).
14. Kompare has written of the American context that 'the heritage is largely constructed, even at the level of "legitimate" history, out of textual artefacts. Television is effectively remembered through its creative and cultural practices, rather than through its industrial practices or social effects' (2005, p. 114).
15. Delivered then by the soon-to-be abolished Museums, Libraries and Archives Council.
16. Though the curators commented that the use of interactive elements resulted in certain difficulties in establishing the behavioural expectations of (especially young) visitors. Given the blurring of interactive elements and display-only exhibits there had been some confusion over what can and can't be touched. A decision was reached to use barriers in the majority of the displays as visitors would often walk straight past the objects in glass boxes.

17. Whilst the framing information emphasises the changing design of the sets across the years, the sets themselves are shuffled within the display: 'For years, the fireplace had been the focal point of the living room. Once the television arrived, this all changed. It gave people a little window on the world in their own homes. Early television sets were huge pieces of furniture. By the 1950s, receivers became smaller and more stylish. As time went on, manufacturers came up with more striking and interesting ways of building televisions. By the 1990s, everything had changed again. Better electronics and bigger screens meant that cabinet design was less important. Increasingly, the focus is on the picture on the screen rather than what's surrounding it' (NMM Gallery of Televisions information card).

18. Greenblatt's other model is 'resonance', referring to the 'power of the displayed object to reach out beyond its formal boundaries to a larger world, to evoke in the viewer the complex, dynamic cultural forces from which it has emerged and for which it may be taken by the viewer to stand' (1990, p. 42).

19. Obviously the financial, material and political realities and constraints on public museums and higher education inevitably curb and curtail forms of pedagogy, but this discussion is about various *possibilities* for exhibiting television and the ways in which the television archive can be employed to engage both visitors and students in different ways.

20. Programmes such as *Cathy Come Home* (BBC, 1966) and *Jamie's School Dinners* (Channel 4, 2005) are cited as examples of the influence of television upon political and social policy and a video loop, narrated by Harry Gration, veteran anchor on regional news programme *Look North* (BBC, 1968–), presents a brief history of television in terms of its sociocultural relevance. Arguably one of the least successful areas of the gallery and one which needs much more work, it currently acts more like a corridor between the main exhibition area and TV Heaven.

21. Alongside historical perspectives, the social impact of television content, the social impact of the television medium and the changing role of television news (National Media Museum Collecting Policy Statement, 2 March 2010). Available at http://www.nationalmediamuseum.org.uk/AboutUs/ReportsPlansPolicies/CollectingPolicy.aspx (accessed 7 February 2011).

22. In Britain, the phasing out of analogue television began in 2005, with the completion of digital switchover in 2012.

Bibliography

Agnew, V. (2007) 'History's affective turn: Historical reenactment and its work in the present', *Rethinking History*, 11.3, 299–312.

Allen, R. C. (1985) *Speaking of Soap Operas* (Chapel Hill, NC: University of North Carolina Press).

Ang, I. (1985) *Watching Dallas: Soap Opera and the Melodramatic Imagination* (London: Methuen).

Anon. (2006) 'Review: *Who Do You Think You Are?*', *Daily Mirror* TV Guide (11 January), p. 19.

Aslama, M. and Pantti, M. (2006) 'Talking alone: Reality TV, emotions and authenticity', *European Journal of Cultural Studies*, 9.2, 167–184.

Bal, M. (1999) 'Memories in the museum: Preposterous histories for today' in M. Bal, J. Crewe and L. Spitzer (eds) *Acts of Memory: Cultural Recall in the Present* (New England: Dartmouth College).

Barthes, R. (2000/1980) *Camera Lucida* (London: Vintage).

Bell, E. and Gray, A. (eds) (2010) *Televising History: Mediating the Past in Post-War Europe* (Houndmills: Palgrave Macmillan).

Benjamin, W. (1999) *Selected Writings Volume 2: 1927–1934* (Cambridge, MA: Harvard University Press (trans. Rodney Livingstone)).

Bennett, J. (2008) 'Television studies goes digital', *Cinema Journal*, 47.3, 158–165.

Biressi, A. and Nunn, H. (2005) *Reality TV: Realism and Revelation* (London: Wallflower).

Boddy, W. (1993) *Fifties Television: The Industry and its Critics* (Chicago, IL: University of Illinois Press).

Bode, S. (ed.) (2007) *Gillian Wearing: Family History* (London: Film and Video Umbrella).

Bode, S., Walwin, J. and Watkins, J. (2007) 'Foreword' in S. Bode (ed.) *Gillian Wearing: Family History* (London: Film and Video Umbrella).

Bondebjerg, I. (1996) 'Public discourse/private fascination: hybridization in "true-life-story" genres' in H. Newcomb (ed.) (2000). *Television: The Critical View*, 6th edn (Oxford: Oxford University Press).

Bourdon, J. (2003) 'Some sense of time: remembering television', *History & Memory*, 15.2, 5–35.

Boym, S. (2001) *The Future of Nostalgia* (New York: Basic Books).

Brown, J. (2001) '*Ally McBeal's* postmodern soundtrack', *Journal of the Royal Musical Association*, 126, 275–303.

Brown, M. (2004) 'Television goes back to its roots', *The Guardian* (13 December) [online]. Available at: http://media.guardian.co.uk/mediaguardian/story/0,7558,1372234,00.html (accessed 25 October 2005).

Brown, S. (1995) *Postmodern Marketing* (London: Routledge).

Brunsdon, C. (2000) 'The structure of anxiety: recent British television crime fiction' in E. Buscombe (ed.) *British Television: A Reader* (Oxford: Oxford University Press).

Brunsdon, C. (2004) 'Taste and time on television', *Screen*, 45.2, 115–129.

Brunsdon, C. (2008) 'Is television studies history?', *Cinema Journal*, 47.3, 127–137.

Brunsdon, C., Johnson, C., Moseley, R. and Wheatley, H. (2001) 'Factual entertainment on British television: The Midlands Television Research Group's "8–9 project" ', *European Journal of Cultural Studies*, 4.1, 29–62.

Bryant, S. (1989) *The Television Heritage* (London: BFI).

Byrne, C. (2005) 'Paxman reduced to tears by journey into his past', *The Independent* (8 December), p. 5.

Caldwell, J. T. (1995) *Televisuality: Style, Crisis and Authority in American Television* (New Brunswick, NJ: Rutgers University Press).

Capote, T. (2000/1980) *Music for Chameleons* (London: Penguin Books).

Cardiff, D. and Scannell, P. (1987) 'Broadcasting and national unity' in J. Curran, A. Smith and P. Wingate (ed.) *Impacts and Influences: Essays on Media Power in the Twentieth Century* (London and New York: Methuen).

Cardwell, S (2005) ' "Television aesthetics" and close analysis: style, mood and engagement in *Perfect Strangers* (Stephen Poliakoff)' in J. Gibbs and D. Pye (eds) *Style and Meaning: Studies in the Detailed Analysis of Film* (Manchester: Manchester University Press).

Caruth, C. (1995) *Trauma: Explorations in Memory* (Baltimore, MD: John Hopkins University).

Caughie, J. (1990) 'Playing at being American: games and tactics' in P. Mellencamp (ed.) *Logics of Television: Essays in Cultural Criticism* (London: BFI).

Caughie, J. (1991) 'Adorno's reproach: repetition, difference and television genre', *Screen*, 32.2, 127–153.

Caughie, J. (2000) *Television Drama: Realism, Modernism and British Culture* (Oxford: Oxford University Press).

Champion, J. (2003) 'Seeing the past: Simon Schama's *A History of Britain* and public history', *History Workshop Journal*, 56, 153–174.

Chapman, J. (2006) *Inside the Tardis: The Worlds of Doctor Who* (London: I.B. Tauris).

Chapman, J. (2009) 'Not "another bloody cop show": *Life on Mars* and British Television Drama', *Film International*, 7.2, 6–19.

Conlan, T. (2010) 'Retailers stop sales of analogue TV sets as digital switchover approaches', *The Guardian* (6 July) [online]. Available at: http://www.guardian.co.uk/media/2010/jul/06/analogue-television-digital-switchover (accessed 7 July 2011).

Conway, B. (2010) *Commemoration and Bloody Sunday* (Houndmills: Palgrave Macmillan).

Cook, P. (2005) *Screening the Past: Memory and Nostalgia in Cinema* (London: Routledge).

Corner, J. (1999) *Critical Ideas in Television Studies* (Oxford: Oxford University Press).

Corner, J. (2006) 'Archive aesthetics and the historical imaginary: *Wisconsin Death Trip*', *Screen*, 47.3, 291–306.

Creeber, G. (2004) *Serial Television* (London: BFI).

Cull, N. J. (2001) ' "Bigger on the inside..." ': *Doctor Who* as British cultural history' in Roberts, G. and Taylor, P. M. (eds) *The Historian, Television and Television History* (Luton: University of Luton Press).

Davies, C. (2007) *Haunted Subjects: Deconstruction, Psychoanalysis and the Return of the Dead* (Hampshire: Palgrave Macmillan).

Dawson, M. (2007) 'Little players, big shows: format, narration, and style on television's new smaller screens', *Convergence*, 13.3, 231–250S.

Day-Lewis, S. (1998) *Talk of Drama: Views of the Television Dramatist Now and Then* (Luton: University of Luton Press).

Deans, J. (2004) 'Oddie found sister through BBC genealogy show', *The Guardian* (28 July) [online]. Available at: http://media.guardian.co.uk/broadcast/story/0,7493,1270988,00.html (accessed 25 October 2005).

de Leeuw, S. (2010) 'Television fiction: a domain of memory – retelling the past on Dutch television' in E. Bell and A. Gray (eds) *Televising History: Mediating the Past in Post-War Europe* (Houndmills: Palgrave Macmillan).

Derrida, J. (1996) *Archive Fever: A Freudian Impression* (Chicago, IL: University of Chicago Press (trans. Eric Prenowitz)).

Doane, M. A. (1990) 'Information, crisis and catastrophe' in P. Mellencamp (ed.) *Logics of Television: Essays in Cultural Criticism* (London: BFI).

Dowell, B. (2007) 'Genealogy show has lost its roots, says expert', *The Guardian* (8 June) [online]. Available at: http://media.guardian.co.uk/bbc/story/0,,2098823,00.html (accessed 27 June 2007).

Downey, C. (2007) '*Life on Mars*, or how breaking the genre rules revitalises the crime fiction tradition', www.crimeculture.com (accessed 6 January 2011).

Dyer, R. (2000/1997) 'To kill and kill again' in J. Arroyo (ed.) *Action/Spectacle Cinema: A Sight and Sound Reader* (London: BFI).

Dyer, R. (2006) *Pastiche* (London: Routledge).

Ebbrecht, T. (2007) 'Docudramatizing history on TV: German and British docudrama and historical event television in the memorial year 2005', *European Journal of Cultural Studies*, 10.1, 35–53.

Ebbrecht, T. (2007) 'History, public memory and media event: Codes and conventions of historical event-television in Germany', *Media History*, 13.2/3, 221–234.

Eco, U. (1990) *The Limits of Interpretation* (Bloomington, IN: Indiana University Press).

Eleftheriotis, D. (2010) *Cinematic Journeys* (Edinburgh: Edinburgh University Press).

Ellis, J. (1982) *Visible Fictions* (London: Routledge).

Elsaesser, T. (1999) ' "One train may be hiding another": private history, memory and national identity', *Screening the Past*, 6 [online]. Available at: http://www.latrobe.edu.au/screeningthepast/classics/rr0499/terr6b.htm (accessed 19 June 2011).

Fiddy, D. (2001) *Missing Believed Wiped: Searching for the Lost Treasures of British Television* (London: BFI).

Freedland, J. (2004) 'Out of the box', *The Guardian* (10 February) [online]. Available at: http://www.guardian.co.uk/g2/story/0,3604,1144522,00.html (accessed 25 November 2004).

Freud, S. (1990) 'The uncanny' in A. Dickson (ed.) *The Penguin Freud Library Volume 14: Art and Literature* (Harmondsworth: Penguin).

Garnett, T. (2000) 'Contexts' in J. Bignell, S. Lacey and M. Macmurraugh-Kavanagh (eds) *British Television Drama: Past, Present and Future* (Hampshire: Palgrave Macmillan).

Garoian, C. R. (2001) 'Performing the museum', *Studies in Art Education*, 42.3, 234–248.

Gauntlett, D. and Hill, A. (1999) *TV Living: Television Culture and Everyday Life* (London: BFI).

Geller, M. (ed.) (1990) *From Receiver to Remote Control: The TV Set* (New York: The New Museum of Contemporary Art).

Geraghty, C. (1981) 'The continuous serial – a definition' in R. Dyer (ed.) *Coronation Street* (London: BFI).

Gilroy, P. (2004) *After Empire: Melancholia or Convivial Culture?* (London: Routledge).

Gilroy, P. (2005) *Postcolonial Melancholia* (New York: Columbia University Press).

Goodwin, C. (2007) 'Just look who's laughing now', *The Sunday Times* (18 August).

Grainge, P. (2002) *Monocrome Memories: Nostalgia and Style in Retro America* (London: Praeger).

Gray, J. (2008) *Television Entertainment* (London: Routledge).

Greenblatt, S. (1990) 'Resonance and Wonder' in Ivan Karp and Steven D. Lavine (eds) *Exhibiting Cultures: The Poetics and Politics of Museum Display* (Washington: Smithsonian Institution Press).

Hanhardt, J. G. (1990) 'The anti-TV set' in M. Geller (ed.) *From Receiver to Remote Control: The TV Set* (New York: The New Museum of Contemporary Art), pp. 111–114.

Hartman, G. (2001) 'Tele-suffering and testimony in the dot com era' in B. Zelizer (ed.) *Visual Culture and the Holocaust* (New Brunswick, NJ: Rutgers University Press).

Haslam, D. (2007) *Young Hearts Run Free: The Real Story of the 1970s* (London: Harper Perennial).

Heath, S. and Skirrow, G. (1977) 'Television, a World in Action', *Screen*, 18.2, 53–54

Hills, M. (2008) 'The dispersible television text: theorising moments of the new *Doctor Who*', *Science Fiction Film and Television*, 1.1, 25–44.

Hirsch, M. (1997) *Family Frames: Photography, Narrative and Post-Memory* (Cambridge, MA: Harvard University Press).

Hirsch, M. (2008) 'The generation of post-memory', *Poetics Today*, 29.1, 103–128.

Hobson, D. (1982) *Crossroads: The Drama of a Soap Opera* (London: Methuen).

Hogg, C. (2010) 'Re-evaluating the archive in Stephen Poliakoff's *Shooting the Past*', *Journal of British Cinema and Television*, 6.3, 437–451.

Holdsworth, A. (2006) 'Slow television and Stephen Poliakoff's *Shooting the Past*', *Journal of British Cinema and Television*, 3.1, 128–133.

Holdsworth, A. (2010) 'Televisual memory', *Screen*, 51.2, 129–142.

Hooper-Greenhill, E. (2000) *Museums and the Interpretation of Visual Culture* (London: Routledge).

Hoskins, A. (2009) 'The mediatisation of memory' in J. Garde-Hansen, A. Hoskins and A. Reading (eds) *Save As . . . Digital Memories* (London: Palgrave Macmillan).

Hunt, T. (2005) 'Whose story?', *The Observer* (19 June) [online]. Available at: http://media.guardian.co.uk/broadcast/story/0,7493,1509770,00.html (accessed 25 November 2005).

Hunt, T. (2007) 'The time bandits', *The Guardian* (10 September) [online]. Available at: http://www.guardian.co.uk/media/2007/sep/10/mondaymediasection. television1 (accessed 17 September 2007).

Hutcheon, L. (1985) *A Theory of Parody: The Teachings of Twentieth-Century Art Forms* (London: Methuen).

Hutcheon, L. (1998) 'Irony, nostalgia and the postmodern'. Available at: www.library.utoronto.ca/utel/criticism/hutchinp.html (accessed 12 November 2005).

Huyssen, A. (1995) *Twilight Memories: Marking Time in a Culture of Amnesia* (London: Routledge).

Huyssen, A. (2003) *Present Pasts: Urban Palimpsests and the Politics of Memory* (Stanford: Stanford University Press).

Jacobs, J. (2001) 'Issues of judgement and value in television studies', *International Journal of Cultural Studies*, 4.4, 427–447.

Jacobs, J. (2003) *Body Trauma TV* (London: BFI).

Jameson, F. (1991) *Postmodernism, or the Cultural Logic of Late Capitalism* (London: Verso).

Jensen, E. (2007) 'New name and mission for Museum of Television', *The New York Times* (5 May) [online]. Available at: http://www.nytimes.com/2007/06/05/arts/design/05pale.html (accessed 5 May 2007).

Johnson, C. (2007) 'Tele-branding in TVIII: the network as brand and the programme as brand', *New Review of Film and Television Studies*, 5.1, 5–24.

Kermode, F. (1967) *The Sense of an Ending* (Oxford and New York: Oxford University Press).

Kerr, P. (2009) '*The Last Slave* (2007): The genealogy of a British television history programme', *Historical Journal of Film, Radio and Television*, 29.3, 381–397.

Kinder, M. (2008) 'Re-wiring Baltimore: The emotive power of systemics, seriality and the city', *Film Quarterly*, 62.7, 50–57.

Klein, K. (2000) 'On the emergence of memory in historical discourse', *Representations*, 69, 127–150.

Kleinecke-Bates, I. (2006) 'Representations of the Victorian age: interior spaces and the detail of domestic life in two adaptations of Galsworthy's *The Forsyte Saga*', *Screen*, 47.2, 139–162.

Kompare, D. (2002) 'I've seen this one before: the construction of "classic TV" on cable television' in J. Thumin (ed.) *Small Screens, Big Ideas: Television in the 1950s* (London: I.B. Tauris).

Kompare, D. (2003) 'Greyish Rectangles: creating the television heritage', *Media History*, 9.2, 153–169.

Kompare, D. (2005) *Rerun Nation* (London: Routledge).

Kuhn, A. (1995) *Family Secrets: Acts of Memory and Imagination* (London: Verso).

Kuhn, A. (2000) 'A journey through memory' in S. Radstone (ed.) *Memory and Methodology* (Oxford: Berg).

Lacey, S. (2006) 'Some thoughts on television history and historiography: a British perspective', *Critical Studies in Television*, 1.1, 3–12.

Landsberg, A. (2004) *Prosthetic Memory* (New York: Columbia University Press).

Lawson, M. (2001) 'Like nothing else', *The Guardian* (7 May). Available at: http://shootingthepast.tripod.com/perfectstrangers/articles/guardian2.htm (accessed 3 March 2005).

Lawson, M. (2004) 'Theories of relativity', *The Guardian* (11 October) [online]. Available at: http://media.guardian.co.uk/broadcast/comment/0, 7493,1324343,00.html (accessed 23 October 2005).

Leal, O. F. (1990) 'Popular taste and erudite repertoire: the place and space of television in Brazil', *Cultural Studies*, 4.1, 19–29.

Lennon, P. (2001) 'No sex, no violence – the viewers will love it', *The Guardian* (3 May). Available at: http://shootingthepast.tripod.com/perfectstrangers/articles/guardian.htm (accessed 3 March 2005).

Leonard, M. (2007) 'Constructing histories through material culture: popular music, museums and collecting', *Popular Music History*, 2.2, 147–167.

Leonard, M. (2010) 'Exhibiting popular music: museum audiences, inclusion and social history', *Journal of New Music Research*, 39.2, 171–181.

Leverette, M., Ott, B. L. and Buckley, C. L. (eds) (2008) *It's Not TV: Watching HBO in the Post-Television Age* (London: Routledge).

Lury, K. (2001) *British Youth Television: Cynicism and Enchantment* (Oxford: Oxford University Press).

Lury, K. (2003) 'Closeup: documentary aesthetics', *Screen*, 44.1, 101–105.

Lury, K. (2005) *Interpreting Television* (London: Hodder Arnold).

Lury, K. (2007) 'A response to John Corner', *Screen*, 48.3, 371–376.

Macdonald, M. (2006) 'Performing memory on television: documentary and the 1960s', *Screen*, 47.3, 327–345.

Macmurraugh-Kavanagh, M. (1999) 'Boys on top: gender and authorship on the BBC Wednesday Play, 1964–70', *Media Culture and Society*, 21.3, 403–425.

Macmurraugh-Kavanagh, M. (2000) 'Too secret for words: coded dissent in female authored Wednesday Plays' in J. Bignell, S. Lacey and M. Macmurraugh-Kavanagh (eds) *British Television Drama: Past, Present and Future* (Houndmills: Palgrave Macmillan).

Maconie, S. (2006) 'Love is all', *Radio Times* (28 October–3 November), p. 18.

Maillet, A. (2004) *The Claude Glass: Use and Meaning of the Black Mirror in Western Art* (New York: Zone Books (trans. Jeff Fort)).

Marc, D. (1984) *Democratic Vistas: Television in American Culture* (Philadelphia, PA: University of Pennsylvania Press).

Marcus, D. (2004) *Happy Days and Wonder Years: The Fifties and the Sixties in Contemporary Cultural Politics* (London: Rutgers University Press).

McCabe, J. and Akass, K. (eds) (2007) *Quality TV: Contemporary American Television and Beyond* (London: I.B. Tauris).

McCarthy, A. (2003) *Ambient Television* (Durham: Duke University Press).

McGrath, J. (2000) 'TV drama: then and now' in J. Bignell, S. Lacey and M. Macmurraugh-Kavanagh (eds) *British Television Drama: Past, Present and Future* (Houndmills: Palgrave Macmillan).

McKee, A (2010) 'YouTube versus the National Film and Sound Archive: Which is the most useful resource for historians of Australian television?', *Television and New Media*, 20.10, 1–20.

McNamara, M. (2010) 'Review: "Who Do You Think You Are?" on NBC', *Los Angeles Times* (5 March) [online]. Available at http://articles.latimes.com/2010/mar/05/entertainment/la-et-who-do-you5-2010mar05 (accessed 2 September 2010).

Meech, P. (1999) 'Watch this space: the on-air marketing communications of UK television', *International Journal of Advertising*, 18.3, 191–304.

Mellencamp, P. (1990) 'TV time and catastrophe, or *Beyond the pleasure principle* of television' in P. Mellencamp (ed.) *Logics of Television: Essays in Cultural Criticism* (London: BFI).

Mitscherlich, A. and Mitscherlich, M. (1975) *The Inability to Mourn: Principles of Collective Behaviour* (New York: Grove Press (trans. Beverly P. Paczek)).

Mittell, J. (2006) 'Narrative complexity in contemporary American television', *The Velvet Light Trap*, 58, 29–40.

Mittell, J. (2008) 'All in the game: *The Wire*, serial storytelling and procedural logic' in P. Harrigan and N. Wardip-Fruin (eds) *Third Person* (Cambridge, MA: MIT Press).

Moran, A. (2009) 'Reasserting the national? Programme formats, international television and domestic culture' in G. Turner and J. Tay (eds) *Television Studies After TV* (London: Routledge).

Moran, J. (2002) 'Childhood and nostalgia in contemporary culture', *European Journal of Cultural Studies*, 5.2, 155–173.

Moran, J. (2004) 'History, memory and the everyday', *Rethinking History*, 8.1, 51–68.

Morley, D. (1986) *Family Television: Cultural Power and Domestic Leisure* (London: Comedia).

Morley, D. (2007) *Media, Modernity and Technology: The Geography of the New* (London: Routledge).

Morse, M. (1990) 'The end of the television reciever' in M. Geller (ed.) *From Receiver to Remote Control: The TV Set* (New York: The New Museum of Contemporary Art).

Muller, A. (2006) 'Notes toward a theory of nostalgia: childhood and the evocation of the past in two European "Heritage" films', *New Literary History*, 37.4, 739–760.

Murdock, G. (1980) 'Authorship and organisation', *Screen Education*, 35, 19–34.

Nelson, J. L. (1990) 'The dislocation of time: a phenomenology of television reruns', *Quarterly Review of Film and Video*, 12.3, 79–92.

Nelson, R. (2006) 'Locating Poliakoff: an auteur in contemporary TV drama', *Journal of British Cinema and Television*, 3.1, 122–127.

Nelson, R. (2007) *State of Play: Contemporary "High End" TV Drama* (Manchester: Manchester University Press).

Newman, K. (2005) *Doctor Who* (London: BFI).

Newman, M. Z. (2006) 'From beats to arcs: towards a poetics of television narrative', *The Velvet Light Trap*, 58, 16–28.

Olin, M. (2002) 'Touching photographs: Roland Barthes's "mistaken" identification', *Representations*, 80, 99–118

O'Sullivan, T. (1991) 'Television memories and cultures of viewing 1950–1965' in J. Corner (ed.) *Popular Television in Britain: Studies in Cultural History* (London: BFI), pp. 159–181.

O'Sullivan, T. (1998) 'Nostalgia, revelation and intimacy: tendencies in the flow of modern popular television' in C. Geraghty and D. Lusted (eds) *The Television Studies Book* (London: Arnold).

Pantti, M. and Van Zoonen, L. (2006) 'Do crying citizens make good citizens?', *Social Semiotics*, 16.2, 205–224.

Parry, R. (2006) *Recoding the Museum: Digital Heritage and the Technologies of Change* (London: Routledge).

Paxman, J. (2006) 'Jeremy Paxman', *Radio Times* (7–13 January), 18–19.

Pickering, J. (1997) 'Remembering D-Day: a case history in nostalgia' in J. Pickering and S. Kehde (eds) *Narratives of Nostalgia, Gender and Nationalism* (London: Macmillan Press).

Pickering, M. and Keightley, E. (2006) 'The modalities of nostalgia', *Current Sociology*, 54.6, 919–941.

Piper, H. (2004) 'Reality television, *Wife Swap* and the drama of banality', *Screen*, 45.4, 273–286.

Plater, A. (2000) 'The age of innocence' in J. Bignell, S. Lacey and M. Macmurraugh-Kavanagh (eds) *British Television Drama: Past, Present and Future* (Houndmills: Palgrave Macmillan).

Polan, D. (2009) *The Sopranos* (Durham: Duke University Press).

Radstone, S. (ed.) (2000) *Memory and Methodology* (Oxford: Berg).

Radstone, S. (2007) *The Sexual Politics of Time: Confession, Nostalgia, Memory* (London: Routledge).

Roberts, G. and Taylor, P. M. (eds) (2001) *The Historian, Television and Television History* (Luton: University of Luton Press).

Root, J. (1990) 'The set in the sitting room' in M. Geller (ed.) *From Receiver to Remote Control: The TV Set* (New York: The New Museum of Contemporary Art) pp. 45–47.

Rowan, D. (2005) 'Interview: Ian Hislop, Private Eye', *Evening Standard* (16 November). Available at: http://www.davidrowan.com/2005/11/interview-ian-hislop-private-eye.html (accessed 10 September 2007).

Saar, M. (2002) 'Genealogy and subjectivity', *European Journal of Philosophy*, 10.2, 231–245.

Sandon, E. (2007) 'Nostalgia as resistance: the case of the Alexandra Palace Television Society and the BBC' in H. Wheatley (ed.) *Re-viewing Television History: Critical Issues in Television Historiography* (London: I.B. Tauris).

Scannell, P. (1996) *Radio, Television and Modern Life* (Oxford: Blackwell).

Schlesinger, P. (2010) ' "The most creative organisation in the world"? The BBC, "creativity" and managerial style', *International Journal of Cultural Policy*, 16.3, 271–285.

Sconce, J. (2000) *Haunted Media* (Durham: Duke University Press).

Sconce, J. (2004) 'What if? Charting television's new textual boundaries' in L. Spigel and J. Olsson (eds) *Television After TV: Essays on a Medium in Transition* (Durham: Duke University Press).

Shattuc, J. (1997) *The Talking Cure: TV, Talk Shows and Women* (London: Routledge).

Sherlock, P. (2010) 'The reformation of memory in early modern Europe' in S. Radstone and B. Schwarz (eds) *Memory: Histories, Theories, Debates* (New York: Fordham University Press).

Silverstone, R. (1994) *Television and Everyday Life* (London: Routledge).

Smit, A. (2010) *Broadcasting the Body: Affect, Embodiment and Bodily Excess on Contemporary Television* (Unpublished PhD Thesis: University of Glasgow).

Sontag, S. (1977) *On Photography* (London: Penguin Classics).

Spicer, G. (2006) 'National Media Museum – A new name and remit for Bradford museum', *24 Hour Museum* (28 November) [online]. Available at: http://www.24hourmuseum.org.uk/nwh_gfx_en/ART41898.html (accessed 7 August 2007).

Spigel, L. (1992a) 'Installing the television set: popular discourses on television and domestic space' in L. Spigel and D. Mann (eds) *Private Screenings: Television and the Female Consumer* (Minneapolis, MN: University of Minnesota Press).

Spigel, L. (1992b) *Make Room for TV: Television and the Family Ideal in Postwar America* (Chicago, IL: Chicago University Press).

Spigel, L. (2001) *Welcome to the Dreamhouse* (Durham: Duke University Press).

Spigel, L. (2004) 'Introduction' in L. Spigel and J. Olsson (eds) *Television After TV: Essays on a Medium in Transition* (Durham: Duke University Press).

Spigel, L. (2005) 'Our TV heritage: television, the archive and the reasons for preservation' in J. Wasko (ed.) *A Companion to Television* (London: Blackwell).

Spigel, L. (2010) 'Housing television: architectures of the archive', *The Communication Review*, 13, 52–74.

Spigel, L. and Curtin, M. (eds) (1997) *The Revolution Wasn't Televised: Sixties Television and Social Change* (London: Routledge).

Steedman, C. (2001) *Dust* (Manchester: Manchester University Press).

Stewart, S. (1993) *On Longing* (Durham: Duke University Press).

Strange, N. (2011) 'Multiplatforming public service: The BBC's "bundled project"' in J. Bennett and N. Strange (eds) *Television as Digital Media* (Durham, NC: Duke University Press).

Sturken, M. (1997) *Tangled Memories: The Vietnam War, the AIDS Epidemic and the Politics of Remembering* (Berkeley, CA: University of California Press).

Sumpner, C., Roberts, R., Armitage, U. and Cross, J. (2005) *Who Do You Think You Are? 360 Audience Feedback*. MC and A: audience and consumer research (for the BBC).

Sutcliffe, T. (2010) 'The weekend's TV', *The Independent* (14 June) [online]. Available at: http://www.independent.co.uk/arts-entertainment/tv/reviews/the-weekends-tv-who-do-you-think-you-are-sun-bbc1brrichard-hammonds-engineering-connections-sun-bbc2-1999546.html (accessed 2 September 2010).

Tannock, S. (1995) 'Nostalgia critique', *Cultural Studies*, 9.3, 453–464.

Taylor, P. M. (2001) 'Television and the future historian' in G. Roberts and P. M. Taylor (eds) *The Historian, Television and Television History* (Luton: University of Luton Press).

Thompson, S. (2005) 'Sky One to trace royal roots of families', *Broadcast Now* (1 December) [online]. Available at: www.broadcastnow.co.uk (accessed 12 January 2006)

Thorpe, V. (2004) 'How Meera Syal traced her revolutionary roots', *The Observer* (10 October) [online]. Available at: http://www.guardian.co.uk/media/2004/oct/10/broadcasting.uknews (accessed October 2005).

Tincknell, E. (2010) 'A sunken dream: music and the gendering of nostalgia in *Life on Mars*' in I. Inglis (ed.) *Popular Music and Television in Britain* (Surrey: Ashgate).

Turim, M. (1989) *Flashbacks in Film* (London: Routledge).

van Dijck, J. (2008) 'Future memories: the construction of cinematic hindsight', *Theory, Culture and Society*, 25.3, 71–87.

Wall to Wall (2006) 'Who Do You Think You Are? forges new roots on BBC ONE' (Press release, 16 February 2006).

Wheatley, H. (2006) *Gothic Television* (Manchester: Manchester University Press).

Wheatley, H. (ed.) (2007) *Re-viewing Television History: Critical Issues in Television Historiography* (London: I.B. Tauris).

Wheeler, W. (1994) 'Nostalgia isn't nasty: the postmodernising of parliamentary democracy' in M. Perryman (ed.) *Altered States: Postmodernism, Politics, Culture* (London: Lawrence and Wishart).

White, M. (2004) 'The attractions of television: reconsidering liveness' in N. Couldry and A. McCarthy (eds) *MediaSpace: Place, Scale and Culture in a Media Age* (London: Routledge).

Whittaker, C. (2001) 'How the BBC pictured itself' in G. Roberts and P. M. Taylor (eds) *The Historian, Television and Television History* (Luton: University of Luton Press).

Williams, R. (1974) *Television: Technology and Cultural Form* (London: Fontana).

Willis, J. (2005) 'John Willis' speech in full', *Broadcast Now* [online]. Available at www.broadcastnow.co.uk (accessed 15 October 2005).

Wilson, R. (2008) 'Remembering to forget? – The BBC Abolition Season and media memory of Britain's transatlantic slave trade', *Historical Journal of Film, Radio and Television*, 28.3, 391–403.

Wolfreys, J. (2002) *Victorian Hauntings: Spectrality, Gothic, the Uncanny and Literature* (Basingstoke: Palgrave Macmillan).

Wollaston, S. (2006) 'Last night's TV', *The Guardian* (10 January) [online] http://www.guardian.co.uk/media/2006/jan/10/broadcasting.tvandradio (accessed 6 September 2010).

Wollaston, S. (2009) 'Last night's TV', *The Guardian* [online] http://www.guardian.co.uk/culture/2009/apr/28/ashes-to-ashes-tv-review (accessed 6 September 2010).

Wood, H. (2009) *Talking With Television: Women, Talk Shows, and Modern Self-Reflexivity* (Urbana, IL: University of Illinois Press).

Wood, H. and Taylor, L. (2008) 'Feeling sentimental about television and audiences', *Cinema Journal*, 47.3, 144–151.

Woods, F. (2007) *Teenage Kicks: Popular Music, Identity and Representation in Teen Film and Television* (Unpublished PhD Thesis: University of Warwick).

Index

Note: Page numbers in **bold** refer to figures.